John P. Jackson

The Ober-Ammerga Passion Play

John P. Jackson

The Ober-Ammerga Passion Play

ISBN/EAN: 9783337376260

Printed in Europe, USA, Canada, Australia, Japan

Cover: Foto ©Thomas Meinert / pixelio.de

More available books at **www.hansebooks.com**

THE OBER-AMMERGAU PASSION PLAY:

[*ILLUSTRATED.*]

GIVING THE ORIGIN OF THE PLAY, AND HISTORY

OF THE VILLAGE AND PEOPLE,

A FULL DESCRIPTION OF

THE SCENES AND TABLEAUX OF THE SEVENTEEN

ACTS OF THE DRAMA,

AND

THE SONGS OF THE CHORUS, IN GERMAN AND ENGLISH.

BY JOHN P. JACKSON,

Author of "*The Album of the Passion Play at Ober-Ammergau*" (1873); *of the English version of* Richard Wagner's *Music Dramas,* "*Rienzi,*" "*Flying Dutchman,*" "*Lohengrin,*" Brüll's "*Golden Cross,*" and Hamerling-Goldschmidt's *Musical Allegory,* "*The Seven Death Sins,*" &c., &c.

LONDON: SOLD BY W. H. SMITH & SON AT THE RAILWAY BOOKSTALLS.

MUNICH (IN COMMISSION): WILLIAM HUMMEL, 20, TURKENSTRASSE.
PARIS: GALIGNANI LIBRARY, 224, RUE DE RIVOLI.
BERLIN: A. ASHER AND CO., 5, UNTER DEN LINDEN.

[*Copyright secured.*]

1880.

PREFACE.

THIS little book is, in the main, a condensation of a larger work, "The Album of the Passion Play," which I published in the year 1873. I have endeavoured to give in a limited space all the information necessary for a proper appreciation of the great religious drama which is attracting so many visitors to the beautiful Highlands of Bavaria. With this thought in mind I have devoted an entire chapter to the life of the villagers of Ober-Ammergau, in order to show that these peasant-actors do not begin their dramatic labours in any hasty or pecuniary spirit. I have described the peculiar religious and dramatic training which the villagers enjoy during the years intervening between one series of decennial performances and another, and which enables them to portray in such an artistic, realistic, and devotional spirit the life and sufferings of the Lord. The remarkable influence which the aged priest-dramatist, the Geistlicher Rath Daisenberger (who still lives) has exerted upon the development of his people and the Passion drama cannot be overlooked by anyone desirous of studying the sacred drama and the peasant-players of Ober-Ammergau.

In the description of the separate acts of the Passion Play I have given the address of the Choragus with which each act is opened, the songs of the Chorus in the original German with English translations, and the essential points of the dialogue spoken by the players. In obtaining the speeches of the Choragus and the text of the drama, I enjoyed peculiar advantages during a lengthy sojourn among the villagers of Ober-Ammergau during and after the performances of the year 1871; indeed, I may say that I am perhaps the only foreigner who has had the privilege of perusing the entire manuscript of the Passion Play, so jealously guarded by the villagers themselves. The complete text of the drama I published in the before-mentioned "Album."

I have not considered it essential to give the various routes to Munich and Ober-Ammergau, since those persons who determine to make the journey will know where to find all the necessary information on this point. I may say, however, that from Munich the railroad carries the traveller in about two hours as far as Murnau, whence it is a distance of only sixteen or seventeen miles to the village of Ober-Ammergau. Those who do not wish to spend much money can take the more popular conveyances, for a few marks; and there are many to whom a walk of sixteen miles, leisurely taken, will be rather a pleasure than otherwise. Still, a carriage drive from Murnau to Ober-Ammergau and back is very delightful.

I would advise the readers of this book, however, not to delay the journey to Ammergau until the Saturday before the performance, and not to leave the village until the next day, or even the day after. A few days' sojourn in the village will prove as pleasant as it is recuperative. The people of Ammergau give a simple welcome to their visitors; the houses and beds are thoroughly clean, and the mountains all about are ever inviting the visitor to excursions. The traveller who "does" the Passion Play in a hurry gets but little enjoyment out of his visit to Ammergau. To those who desire to become acquainted with the every-day life of the people, and to take away with them a delightful record of a residence in the village, I would recommend Mrs. Greatorex's book entitled "The Homes of Ober-Ammergau," with etchings of the dwelling-places of the principal actors of the Passion Play.

J. P. J.

LONDON,
May 8th, 1880.

LIST OF THE PRINCIPAL PERFORMERS IN 1871 AND 1880.

	1871.	1880.
CHRIST	*Joseph Maier*	*Joseph Maier.*
PETER	*Jacob Hett*	*Jacob Hett.*
JOHN	*Johannes Zwink*	*Johannes Zwink.*
VIRGIN MARY	*Franziska Flunger*	*Anastasia Krach.*
MARY MAGDALENE	*Josepha Lang*	*Maria Lang.*
HEROD	*Franz Paul Lang*	*Johann Rutz.*
PILATE	*Tobias Flunger*	*Thomas Rendl.*
JUDAS	*Gregor Lechner*	*Gregor Lechner.*
CAIAPHAS	*Johann Lang*	*Johann Lang.*
ANNAS	*Gregor Stadler*	*Seb. Deschler.*
NATHANIEL	*Paul Fröschl*	*Seb. Lang.*
EZEKIEL	*Sebastian Deschler*	*Rochus Lang.*
JOSEPH OF ARIMATHEA	*Thomas Rendl*	*Martin Oppenrieder.*
NICODEMUS	*Anton Haafer*	*Franz Steinbacher.*
BARABBAS	*Johann Allinger*	*Johann Allinger.*
CHORAGUS	*Johann Diemer*	*Johann Diemer.*
CONDUCTOR	*Jos. Al. Kirschenhofer*	*Jos. Al. Kirschenhofer.*

THE ROYAL BAVARIAN STAINED GLASS
MANUFACTORY OF F. X. ZETTLER.

STAINED GLASS WINDOWS OF EVERY DESCRIPTION.

SHOW ROOMS OPEN DAILY, EXCEPT SUNDAY,
From 9 till 12, and 2 till 6 o'clock.

MUNICH:
MARSSTRASSE, 12, NEAR THE CENTRAL RAILWAY STATION.

BERNESE OBERLAND. INTERLAKEN, SWITZERLAND.
INTERNATIONAL RENDEZVOUS OF TOURISTS
FROM ALL PARTS OF THE WORLD.
MOST CELEBRATED CLIMATERIC HEALTH RESORT.
ALTITUDE 1,800 FEET ABOVE SEA.

CENTRAL STATION and Starting Point for all Excursions to the grand region of the ALPS and Glaciers of the world-famed BERNESE OBERLAND. Beautiful change of scenery according to each season. Splendid floral period in the Spring season—from April to June. In the Summer season —from July to August—the temperature is always moderate, owing to the refreshing breezes from both lakes; whilst in the lovely Autumn season—from September to October—the air is the purest, the temperature warm, and the vegetation in its full growth. **Whey and Grape Cure.** Magnificent alleys of chestnut trees, and shady walks. Park-maze in the Rugen Pine Woods. Numerous Hotels, from the luxurious Grand Hôtel to the nice wooden Châlet; Private Apartments to all requirements. Special Protestant, English, Scotch Presbyterian, and Roman Catholic Churches. The Curhouse (Park Garden) is the centre of reunion of all visitors, and contains Dancing, Concert, and Reading Rooms, with a well-compiled Library. Choicest selections played daily by the superior Cur-orchestra. The Prices in the Hotels and Boarding-Houses are not higher, but rather lower, than in most other frequented places. The annual average of visitors is upwards of 100,000.

Name	Type	Class	Rooms	Proprietor
Victoria	Gd. Hôtel	1st Class	230	ED. RUCHTI.
Ritschard	,,	,,	235	FAMILIE RITSCHARD.
Jungfrau	,,	,,	150	F. SEILER-STERCHI.
Des Alpes	,,	,,	180	JB. MAURER.
Rugenhotel Jungfraublick	,,	,,	100	J. ORSCH-MÜLLER.
Beau-Rivage	,,	,,	100	H. REGLI.
Schweizerhof	Hôtel and Pension	,,	80	STRUBIN & WIRTH.
Belvedere	,, ,,	,,	70	M. MÜLLER-STÆHLI.
Interlaken	,, ,,	2nd Class	80	A. BRAUEN.
Deutscherhof	,, ,,	,,	70	J. BORTER-RUBIN.
Ober-Béha	,, ,,	,,	60	WWE OBER-BÉHA.
Du Nord	,, ,,	,,	50	DL. VOGEL.
Wyder	,, ,,	,,	60	H. WYDER.
Beau-Site	,, ,,	,,	80	ALB. RUCHTI.
Oberland	,, ,,	,,	50	WAGNER.
Du Pont	,, ,,	,,	50	BRUNNER TSCHANZ.
Bellevue	,, ,,	,,	40	ELMER.
Adler	,, ,,	,,	20	KERNEN.
De la Gare	...	,,	30	E. HALLER.
Kreuz	Hôtel	,,	25	F. BOHREN-STRUBIN.
Rössli	Hôtel and Pension	3rd Class	20	F. STERCHI.
Volz	Pension	...	24	DR. VOLZ.
Reber	,,	...	20	GUTZCHEBAUCH.
Berger	Hôtel and Pension	2nd Class	15	BERGER.
Pension Anglaise	...	...	20	E. SIMPKIN.
Krebs	Hôtel and Pension	2nd Class	15	KREBS-BORTER.
Indermühle	Brasserie-Restaurant, 1st Class Establishment.			

OBER-AMMERGAU, SEEN FROM THE PASSION THEATRE.

PLAN OF THEATRE AND PRICES.

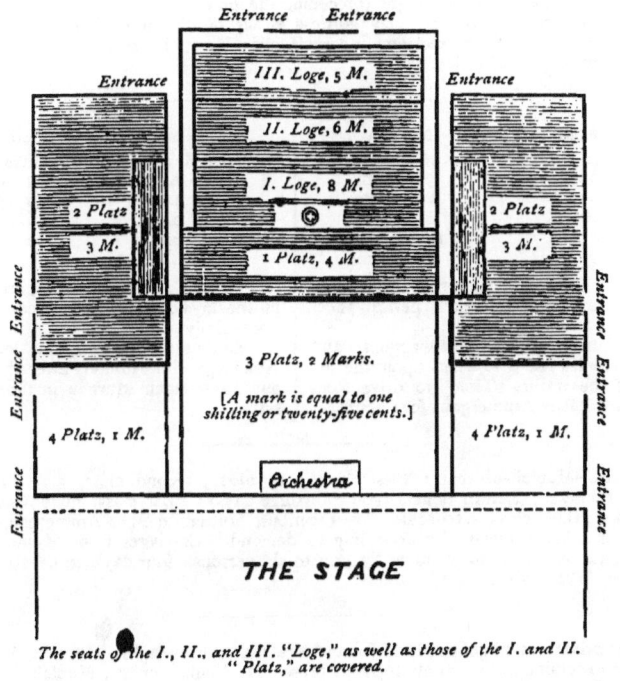

The seats of the I., II., and III. "Loge," as well as those of the I. and II. "Platz," are covered.

DATES OF PERFORMANCES.

The performances take place this year on the following days :—

Monday,	May	17.	Sunday,	July	25.
Sunday,	,,	23.	Sunday,	Aug.	1.
Sunday,	,,	30.	Sunday,	,,	8.
Sunday,	June	6.	Sunday,	,,	15.
Sunday,	,,	13.	Sunday,	,,	22.
Wednesday,	,,	16.	Sunday,	,,	29.
Sunday,	,,	20.	Sunday,	Sept.	5.
Thursday,	,,	24.	Wednesday,	,,	8.
Sunday,	,,	27.	Sunday,	,,	12.
Sunday,	July	4.	Sunday,	,,	19.
Sunday,	,,	11.	Sunday,	,,	26.
Sunday,	,,	18.			

When, on any of the above days, the number of visitors is greater than can be accommodated in the auditorium, the play will be repeated (in full) the day following.

The performance commences at 8 a.m. and continues till 5 p.m., with one hour's intermission (at noon).

Visitors usually pass the night (preceding the play) at Ober-Ammergau. To secure lodgings and tickets for the play address either of the following persons in Ober-Ammergau: Herrn Bürgermeister, Johann Lang; Herrn Beigeordneter, Joseph Mayer; Herrn Pfarrer, J. N. Müller.

RAILROAD: MUNICH—MURNAU.		RAILROAD: MURNAU—MUNICH.	
Leave Munich.	Arrive Murnau.	Leave Murnau:	Arrive Munich.
6 20 a.m.	9 55 a.m.	4 0 a.m.	7 40 a.m.
10 45 a.m.	2 30 p.m.	10 30 a.m.	2 15 p.m.
2 30 p.m.	6 10 p.m.	2 55 p.m.	6 40 p.m.
6 30 p.m.	10 15 p.m.	6 30 p.m.	10 5 p.m.
*1 50 p.m.	4 5 p.m.	*9 10 p.m.	11 25 p.m.

The last * is a special train, and runs only on the day preceding each performance. The other trains daily.

Omnibuses, stages, post-waggons, and other vehicles leave Murnau upon the arrival of the trains. Time (to drive from Murnau to Ober-Ammergau) four hours.

The last * is a special train, and runs only on the days of the performance. The other trains daily.

Omnibuses, stages, &c., leave Ober-Ammergau immediately after the performance, and reach Murnau in time for the * train.

Fares—Munich-Murnau: First class, 6.15 Mks.; second class, 4.10 Mks.; third class, 2.60 Mks. Return tickets (good for three days): First class, none; second class, 6.15 Mks.; third class, 4.10 Mks. Post Omnibus, Murnau to Ober-Ammergau, 2.60 Mks. Prices for other vehicles vary according to demand. Carriages from Munich to Ober-Ammergau, and back to Munich, for one to six persons: four day's trip, 120 Mks.; five days, 140 Mks.; six days, 160 Mks.

For private carriages apply to Johann Kratzer, 7, Frauen Pl., Munich.
For excursion tickets apply to Alois Mössl, 11, Neuhauser St., Munich.
For English books, &c., apply to B. Wahnschaffe, 8, Brienner St., Munich.

U.S. CONSULATE, MUNICH,
    May, 1880.

THE PILGRIMAGE.

THE attention of the Christian world is again drawn to the remarkable drama of the Passion, performed by the villagers of Ober-Ammergau, in the highlands of Bavaria. Tradition says that the celebrated religious play, which is now given every tenth year, dates as far back as 1634, being now performed in fulfilment of a solemn vow made then to God by the villagers. The tradition is as follows:—In the year 1633 a fearful pestilence broke out in the neighbouring villages; so fearful, indeed, it was thought everybody would die. In Kohlgrub, distant three hours' journey from Ammergau, so great were the ravages made by the disease, that only two married couples were left in the village. Notwithstanding the strict measures taken by the people of Ammergau to prevent the plague being introduced into their village, a day labourer, named Caspar Schuchler, who had been working at Eschenlohe, where the plague prevailed, succeeded in entering the village, where he wished to visit his wife and children. In a day or two he was a corpse: he had brought with him the germs of the disease, which spread with such fearful rapidity that, within the following thirty-three days, eighty-four persons belonging to the village died. Then the villagers, in their sad trial, assembled, and solemnly vowed that, if God would take away the pestilence, they would perform the Passion Tragedy in thanksgiving every tenth year. From that time on, although a number of persons were suffering, not one more died of the plague. In 1634 the play was first performed. The decadal period was chosen for 1680, and the Passion Play has been enacted every tenth year, with various interruptions, since that time.

Such is the current tradition. The Passion Play is, however, of much older date than this. It is not probable that simple villagers would make a vow to perform a play totally unknown to them, and, even in its rudest form, demanding such capacity and preparatory study. The vow speaks of the Passion Tragedy as something well known; only the period of performing the play every ten years is positively stated. The oldest known text-book of the play bears the date 1662, and it refers to a still older book. Since the year 1634 the Passion Play has undergone great changes and improvements. Such figures as Lucifer, Prince of Hell, who, with his retinue, used to play a great part in the Ammergau performance, have been banished. The devil was formerly a constant actor upon the stage; for instance, he used to dance about Judas during the course of the latter's temptation, and when the betrayer hanged himself, a host of satanic imps would rush upon the suicide, and tear open his bowels, to find a good meal of very palatable sausages or other savoury material. Up to the year 1830 the play was performed in the village churchyard, in the open air. In the first decades of the present century the text of the Play was thoroughly revised by Father Ottmar Weiss, of Jesewang, ex-conventual of the Benedictine Monastery at Ettal (died 1843), who removed unsuitable and inharmonious passages, substituting prose for doggrel verse. The improvements then commenced have been carried on up to the present time by the former pastor of the village, the Geistlicher-Rath Daisenberger, who is still active in promoting the success of the play.

The last performances of the Passion Play were given in the year 1871. The performances of 1870 (the decadal year) had been suddenly interrupted by the breaking-out of the Franco-German war, when the Passion Theatre had to be closed long before the stipulated term, and the visitors were scattered like chaff to the four winds. Forty of the men and youth of Ammergau, among them several who had taken part in the play, were called into the ranks of the Bavarian army. Joseph Maier, the delineator of the person of Christ in 1870, was among the number of those who had to perform military duty, though it fortunately happened that the King of Bavaria, Ludwig II., who had ever manifested a deep interest in the Passion Play, interfered in his favour, commanding that, instead of doing active service in the field, he should be allowed to fulfil his duties in the Munich garrison. None of the other principal players were called to the ranks. Of the forty who left the village in 1870 for the war, six never returned from France: of these, two fell in battle and four died in the hospitals. Alois Lang, one of the six victims of the war, had undertaken, before he left his native village, the part of Simon of Cyrene. When the news of peace between Germany and France arrived in the Bavarian Highlands, and fires of joy were lighted on every mountain-top, from the Odenwald to the Tyrol, the good villagers of Ober-Ammergau met together, for the purpose of joining in the general expression of triumph and exultation. "With the permission of our gracious sovereign," they said, "we will give a repetition of our Passion Play. This shall be our method of thanking God, who has bestowed upon us the blessings of victory and peace!"

The invitation to attend the performances found acceptance far beyond the borders of Germany. The fame of the play of 1870 had spread into all Christian lands; and when it was known that the performances would be repeated in 1871, Ammergau became the goal towards which the great body of tourists directed their steps. The journey was then, as it is in the present year, for many a true Passion pilgrimage. The village of Ober-Ammergau is far removed from the noise of the great world, and a long day's journey, attended with no little exertion, has to be made from Munich before it is reached. Leaving the Bavarian capital, the traveller has the choice of several routes. One of these is by the railroad to Starnberg, and along the shores of the lake of the same name to Murnau. A four hours' drive from this place in a carriage or omnibus completes the journey to the village. Those who prefer crossing the beautiful Lake Starnberg can take the steamer from Starnberg to Seeshaupt, and thence by conveyance to Ammergau. In the journey by railroad, every mile possesses interest to the tourist. There is a wealth of legendary lore stored among the peasant populations through which the road passes. Planegg, a few stations distant from the Bavarian capital, is celebrated as a place of pilgrimage, the great object of attraction being the Virgin's Oak, with its image of the Madonna, of wide-spread miraculous reputation. In the Mühlthal, the tradition of the birth of Charlemagne lends an historical interest to the neighbourhood. At a short distance further the first glimpse of Lake Starnberg is obtained. It is a beautiful, placid sheet of water, speckled with the white sails of yachts, and ploughed occasionally by a steamer from the little town of Starnberg, across its whole length to the many charming villages that dot its shores. It is a pleasant sail across the blue waters, past idyllic villas and mansions, among which Schloss Berg, one of the favourite residences of Ludwig II., is conspicuous; past the Garden of Roses, one of the many artificial paradises which the romantic monarch has created in or near his residences; past Leoni, a place hallowed by artistic memories; past the legendary St. Heinrich, until the bell announces that Seeshaupt is reached. " Beautiful Starnberg !" are the words that escape the traveller's lips as he first catches a glimpse of the lake; and " Beautiful Starnberg !" when he bids it adieu for the more romantic pleasures of the beckoning snow-crowned mountains. The shores of the lake are a paradise which the Munich artists well know how to enjoy, and where they celebrate many of their annual festivals, for which the German artists are justly celebrated. Characteristic of the fruitful scene were the words of the hordes of Attila, who, when they overran Bavaria, shouted, "To Bayern! To Bayern! There dwells the Lord God himself!"

Between the lake, where we have so long tarried, and the Bavarian Highlands, there lies a broad plain of several miles in extent. Those tourists who prefer the overland transit, proceed by train either to Murnau or to Sulz, at the foot of a mountain called the High Peissenberg, which has merited the name of the Bavarian Righi. But of late years it seems to possess less attractions for the traveller than it formerly did. The greater number of Passion pilgrims keep the rails as far as Murnau. If we may believe tradition, the little town was originally named, with the valley which it overlooks, Wurmau, *i.e.* the Valley of the Dragon. Murnau had a Passion Play in earlier times. A charming lake, the Staffelsee, lies near the village. Crowning one of the islands is a small Kapelle which tradition says was consecrated by Saint Boniface, the great apostle of the Germans. After leaving Murnau, we pass on our way to Ammergau through the valley of the Loisach. The road passes between shady rows of trees; beside us, the little river glides smoothly along, unencumbered in summer, but in winter destined to carry down from the mountains its burden of floats. Rising majestically in front, are the high peaks of the mountains, crowned with snow up to late in the summer. To the right is the Etaller range, with the Etaller-Mandl, over five thousand feet, and to the left the Herzogenstand and the Krottenkopf, about six thousand feet high ; while directly in front, apparently barring the end of the gorge, is the Zugspitze, near Garmisch, with a height of nearly ten thousand feet. At length the traveller's path itself is closed in by the lofty ranges on either side, so that space is scarcely left between the mountain and the opposite mass of precipitous rocks, for the two slender lines of road and river. During the Passion season the road is animated, one or even two days before the performance, by the numbers of conveyances and by the picturesque groups of foot-passengers. With what resoluteness of purpose, and with what devotion of spirit do many of these poor peasants undertake the journey! See them, long before their destination is reached, climb up the sides of the little mount near Eschenlohe, in order to join the groups of the devout, who never cease to invoke the Madonna, in the beautiful "Gnadenkapelle," or chapel of grace, which crowns its summit. Sanctuaries of this kind, containing an image of the Virgin, of miraculous fame, seem to have been planted on every knoll of the valley. A reader of Uhland would not be able to pass beneath these chapel-crowned mounts without repeating the beautiful verses of that poet entitled: "Die Kapelle." Let him substitute the cow-boy or the goat-herd boy of the Loisach valley for the shepherd-boy of Suabia, and the picture is complete :—

> On the height the chapel clinging, reigning o'er a vale of joy,
> Down 'mid brook and meadow singing, loud and glad the shepherd boy!
>
> Sadly sounds the bells' deep tolling ; full of dread the burial lay :
> Now no more his glad song trolling, looks the youngling in dismay.
>
> Up there to the grave they're bringing, those who dwelt down in the vale:
> Soon, boy shepherd, they'll be singing, for thee there, thy funeral wail!

How fortunate is it, that the great Etaller Berg has been placed between the highway leading from Murnau to Partenkirchen, the valley of the Ammer and the village of Ober-Ammergau. For to this barrier we are indebted for one circumstance of inestimable value. The actors of the Passion Play, cut off by their geographical position from communication with the outer world, have escaped its contaminating influences ; and are able, after the lapse of so many decades, to exhibit their sacred drama in more than its original purity. When the tourist comes to the little village of Oberau, he finds that the distinction of persons ceases for a while ; rich and poor have to struggle with the steepness of Mount Ettal for over half-an-hour, while a pair of the best horses are tugging hard to draw up the empty carriage. Half-way up the steep hill the tourist is struck by one of those votive tablets, so common in these parts. It tells the story of Alois Pfausler, who here met a

THE MONASTERY OF ETTAL.

sudden death from apoplexy in July, 1866, brought on by his over-exertion in climbing the hill. A little further on, to the right, some wooden steps lead to a sanctuary of the Madonna, where the devout spend a few moments in rest and prayer. Nearly at the top of the hill is a monument, made of granite, erected to the memory of F. X. Hauser, master stone-mason of Munich, and his foreman Jos. Kofelens, who were both killed by the falling of the statue of St. John on its transport to Ober-Ammergau, where it forms part of the "Krenzignosgsgruppe." The good people of the neighbourhood firmly believe in the old proverb, current in the Ammer valley, that "the way to the representation of the Passion Play should be a way of penance."

But the toil once surmounted, and the summit reached, the pilgrim stands in full view of a surprising scene of beauty, which marks the entrance to the Ammerthal. Here the ancient Benedictine Monastery of Ettal nestles beneath the Ettaler-Mandl, whose peak is discernible even at Murnau. Ettal is the guardian of the valley through which Ober-Ammergau is reached. The monastery, as such, is no more, and the monks who once inhabited it have long since departed to their eternal rest. Ettal is one of the many wonderful sites noted for incomparable beauty, which the sons of Saint Benedict were wont to select for their abode. Devrient was one of the first to assert that the Ammergau Passion Play came originally from Ettal. But the aged priest of Ober-Ammergau, Geistlicher Rath Daisenberger, editor of the Passion Play in its present form, is of a contrary opinion. His arguments, however, do not seem conclusive. He says, truly, that at the time of the great pestilence (1633) Ober-Ammergau stood under the pastoral charge of the monastery of Rothenbuch, five or six leagues distant from the place, but not in the same direction as Ettal. The prelates of that monastery were feudal lords of the valley, and exercised secular jurisdiction in the neighbourhood, but at first they had no influence in spiritual matters. Even Daisenberger admits, however, that the monks of Ettal may have aided the villagers in carrying out their vow. Dr. Holland is of the opinion that the Passion Play was introduced into Ammergau simultaneously with the craft of woodcarving. For both acquisitions, he thinks, they were indebted to the monks of Rothenbuch. The date which he gives is the twelfth century. And, indeed, as to the supposition that the Passion Play dates from the pestilence of 1633, we have already hinted that it is totally unfounded. Leaving, however, to Rothenbuch the credit of having first prepared the text and introduced the religious drama into Ober-Ammergau, it is probable that as soon as the monastery of Ettal was established, the latter took the immediate guidance of any existing dramatic elements into their own hands. That both the monks of Rothenbuch and of Ettal had religious plays cannot be controverted; for in 1803, when the property of the suppressed Bavarian monasteries was put up at auction, costumes used in the religious plays were sold, and the community of Ober-Ammergau purchased from Ettal a number of dresses, some of which they still turn to use.

Ever since its foundation Ettal has been, like Alt Oetting and Berg Andechs in Bavaria, and like Maria Einsiedeln in Switzerland, a noted place of pilgrimage, to which thousands upon thousands repair, not only from the surrounding country, but even from more remote districts, in order to perform their devotions before the shrine of the Madonna of miraculous fame. This statue was guarded by the monks from the infancy of their institute, and all along during the time of their prosperity; and it is still faithfully preserved by the curates, who have succeeded to their functions. Ettal is, indeed, so closely connected with Ammergau in life and religion, that a glimpse of its history belongs to any account of the Passion Play. Besides their principal drama, the villagers of Ober-Ammergau have a secular play, which they frequently perform, entitled " The Founding of the Monastery of Ettal," written by the Geistlicher Rath Daisenberger. The German Emperor, Ludwig the Bavarian, after having been crowned in Rome, found himself suddenly attacked near Milan. While in the monastery of Saint Victor, imploring aid in his distress, a monk appeared, and placing in his hands a beautiful image of the Virgin, promised him the divine blessing if he would pledge himself, on arriving in the valley of the Ammer, to found a Benedictine monastery, and place in it the image for public veneration. This he promised, and fulfilled after he had escaped from his enemies. Tradition says that the emperor rode his horse up the same steep Ettaler Berg, which the pilgrim now ascends with so much toil: but no sooner had he gained the upper part, than the animal fell three times in succession upon its knees, unable to carry the imperial weight which it bore any further. The emperor interpreted this incident as a sign from heaven, which it was not permitted to neglect, and here, at the entrance of the valley where he had received such a marked intimation of the divine will, he determined that his vow should be put into execution. Accordingly he ordered a small chapel to be hastily constructed; and, in the year 1330, he made the journey from Munich in order to lay the foundation stone of the monastery of Ettal.

Having once laid the foundation stone, Ludwig continued to take great interest in the prosperity of his own creation. And, indeed, " under the protection of the Queen of Heaven," whom he regarded as the principal foundress, it soon began to flourish. But the edifice which the emperor erected was not to be a mere dwelling-place for monks: it was also to serve as a retreat for incapacitated knights and warriors, who would have no other duty but to guard the image of the Madonna, who had in a wonderful manner brought him aid in the time of distress. We see that a bright image, that of the Holy Grail, which in the history of Christian poetry has something of a universal character, had made a lively impression upon his mind. It was a Grail Temple—this foundation of Ludwig the Bavarian. His father, Ludwig the Austere, had manifested a disposition favourable to the ideal side of literature. It was at his command that the epic poem of " Titurel," which, however, remained in an imperfect state, had been composed by Wolfram of Eschenbach. Among the fine passages which this production contains, there is a grand description of the Holy Grail, and of the Castle of Monsalvat, the legendary home of Parcival and Lohengrin. What the latter had caused to spring up in the shape of fiction, the former determined to realize as one of the institutions of his kingdom. For this purpose he created, as we may interpret his notion, a clerical order of knighthood. Ettal was his Monsalvat, and the monks were the knights of the Grail. The palladium of which the monks became the depositaries, was not the Holy Grail, but the cherished statue, which had brought the emperor unexpected relief, in the Chapel of the Madonna, near Milan. Towards the end of his life, after his unhappy rupture with the occupant of the papal chair, the emperor, depressed in spirit by the anathema which he had incurred, seems to have taken a melancholy pleasure in spending much of his time in his barge on a neighbouring lake, called the Plansee. There, giving full scope to his romantic turn of mind, he might perchance imagine, that he was acting an episode out of Wolfram's "Parcival," that he was himself the benighted king whose wounds were incurable, that like another Anfortas on the waters of the Brumbane, while he could not live, he was nevertheless doomed not to die. Ettal, as it now stands, bears few traces of the original plan, both church and monastery having been subsequently destroyed by fire and lightning. Yet by comparing actual remains with descriptions of the original structure, as given by eye-witnesses, we gain sufficient evidence that there was a great resemblance between the stone architecture of Ludwig the Bavarian and the lofty rhyme built up by Wolfram, which served as a model. Substituting, as we have already done, the image of the Virgin for the vessel of the Holy Grail, we might almost believe that Wagner had the abbey of Ettal in view when he made the description of the legendary home of Lohengrin:—

In distant land, where ye can never enter,	A precious vessel, of miraculous power,
A castle stands, the Monsalvat its name!	A shrine most holy, guarded well, doth stand;
A radiant temple riseth in the centre,	That none but mortals purest guard this dower,
More beauteous 'tis than aught of earthly fame!	'Twas brought to earth by an angelic hand!

In 1744 the abbey, the church, and the library were laid in ashes by a single stroke of lightning; and nearly all the treasures were destroyed. The prior, however, succeeded in rescuing the statue at the risk of his own life. After 1744 the church was restored. In 1803 Ettal was involved in the common ruin of all monastic corporations in Bavaria, and its inmates wandered to other homes and distant lands. Ettal is now noted, besides its Madonna, for its beautiful organ and its beer. The fresco paintings on the roof of the church, by Jacob Zeiller, of Reutte, and those in the spaces above the altars, by Martin Knoller, an artist from the Tyrol, still attract the attention of the tourist. In association with the Madonna and the organ, they are the only relics which Ettal still preserves of its pristine splendour, and of the treasures which were gathered within its walls during the four hundred years of its prosperity. Attempts have been made at times to induce the government to rebuild the monastery as a college, and the late King Maximilian showed a willingness to enter into such a project. He even caused some preparations to be made towards its realization: but after his death they were suffered to fall.

Leaving the portal and the precincts of the church at Ettal and the whole of this elevated region, and entering the lovely valley of the Ammer, the pilgrim can well appreciate the sentiments of good old Ethiko,—in the drama of the "Founding of Ettal,"—as he leaves his solitary cell in the early spring-time, and blesses God for all the goodness he has spent in such wealth in the valley, and can join with the players of Ober-Ammergau in singing the closing words thereof (by the Geistlicher Rath Daisenberger):—

Let God be praised! He hath this vale created,
To show to man the glory of His name!
And these wide hills the Lord hath consecrated,
Where He His love incessant may proclaim!

In this close valley, from the world divided,
Where rock and pine point upward to the sky,
By fervent prayer, man's soul to God is guided,
Whom in His works he strives to glorify.

From out these aisles will flow Maria's blessing,
Far through the vales of this our Fatherland!
I see, in spirit, thousands onward pressing,
As one in faith, a pious pilgrim band.

On holy ground, in worship humbly kneeling,
The soul by hope stirr'd deeply, and by love,
I see the poor, life's sorest troubles feeling,
Forget their ills in comfort from above!

And happy ones, I see, for grace are pleading,
And off'rings pleasing unto God they bring;

And princes, too, the voice of warning heeding,
In meekness bend before their Lord and King.

And youths who have from distant lands departed,
Assemble here — for wisdom's fount athirst;
For in these halls shall comfort be imparted,
Maternally, the sacred wisdom nursed!

And when in course of time, as man's creation,
Good Ludwig's house a shatter'd ruin lies;
Its memory be kept aye in veneration,
Until, renew'd, it may once more arise!

Ne'er shall decay the valley's greatest treasure,
Madonna—thou—the pledge of Heaven's grace!
Her blessings will the Queen of Heaven outmeasure
To her quiet Ettal and Bavaria's race!

O Mother, stay with us,—thy love unswerving,—
Reign over us, maternally, sublime!
To Bayern's people, princes, too, preserving,
Good Heaven's grace throughout the course of time!

An hour's walk through the delightful valley, along the banks of the mountain stream from which it derives its name, leads the tourist to the village of Ober-Ammergau. Two rows of mountain ash, hung with clusters of rich red berries, mark the line of the valley-road during its whole extent, until we come to the place of destination. Here our attention is forcibly drawn to the bold and curiously formed peak of the Kofel, crowned with a large cross. It rises immediately in front of the village, and the latter lies nestling below it. The first object, which a turn in the road reveals to the eye of the pilgrim, is the village church with its peculiar dome, not unlike that of a Turkish mosque. Just before entering the village, on a prominent point of the valley

MARBLE GROUP OF THE CRUCIFIXION.

Presented to the community of Ober-Ammergau, by King Ludwig II. of Bavaria, in commemoration of His Majesty's visit to Ober-Ammergau to witness the Passion Play in 1871, and his appreciation of the earnest labours of the villagers in the performance of the vow made by their forefathers in the year 1633.

is a marble group representing a scene of the Crucifixion,—Christ nailed to the Cross and the Virgin and John standing at the foot, at the moment when the Redeemer says to His mother: "Woman, behold thy son!" and to the disciple, "Behold, thy mother!" This is the gift of King Ludwig to the villagers of Ober-Ammergau, in commemoration of the performances of 1871. The work is by Halbig, of Munich. A more appropriate monument for the lovely valley of the Ammer could not have been chosen.

Ober-Ammergau has the reputation of being one of the cleanest villages in the Bavarian Highlands. The sparkling Ammer rushing along the streets, the deep shadows of the lofty Kofel, and those of the high ranges all around, render it one of the most picturesque of situations. The peak of the Kofel, with its cross, is the presiding genius of the place. Long before the sun sends his rays down into the valley, the high cross is radiant with golden light, and when the orb of day sinks to rest, it reflects the last faint glow of his vanishing light. It once happened that, either in jest or earnest, a proposal was made to the Ammergauers to take their Passion Play to England or America. "Willingly will we do so," was the reply, "but we must take with us the whole village, and its guardian spirit, the Kofel." So vivid is the impression which this venerable peak has engraved on their minds.

VILLAGE AND PEOPLE.

THE great object of interest connected with Ammergau is unquestionably the Passion Play. But as it is impossible fully to understand and appreciate the nature of such a performance without becoming in some way acquainted with the performers, we shall be justified in casting a glance at their manners and customs, and at their preparations for the labours they religiously undertake. Many influences have been at work to produce the marvellous peasant-players of Ammergau. The first of these is the ceremonial life of the church, and in close connection with this the skill of the villagers in wood-carving. All the more intelligent and better educated members of the community are wood-carvers; and the subjects which they execute by preference are of the religious kind—crucifixes, madonnas, images of saints, and church ornaments. The influence exercised by wood-carving upon the villagers is seen in the improvement of taste, and in the preparation of the people for the part of the figures they act on the stage. They have gradually acquired a feeling for correctness of form and fitness of pose. What they cut out in wood, they represented on the stage. Many of these workmen deserve the name of artists. The past generation had not the advantage of an artistic training. Some of the old men belonging to this period who still survive, are unable to draw on paper the subjects which they carry out with much delicacy in wood, and the characteristic style of productions is more traditional than learned.

Happily, the Bavarian government has endeavoured to aid the villagers in their aspirations, and to facilitate their progress in these artistic pursuits. The School of Design and Carving which is established in the neighbouring town of Partenkirchen, receives an annual subvention from the State. The Ammergau School of Design, situated in the village itself, is well attended ; and the inhabitants do not shrink from sacrifices in order to support it. The best players of the village are, almost without exception, wood-carvers, and this in the higher branches. The three men who have represented " Christus " since the beginning of 1850, Flunger, Schauer, and Maier, were all distinguished in this profession. Of these, the first devoted his skill chiefly to madonnas, and the two others to crucifixes. Besides their principal employment, Flunger dedicates some of his spare hours to animal carving, and Maier a portion of his leisure to flowers and picture-frames. Jacob Hett, the "Petrus" of 1870, is a carver of small crucifixes. Lechner, the admirable personator of Judas, is one of the most skilful carvers of the village, as he is one of the very first of the actors. The peasants, or agricultural labourers, are not fitted for the higher characters. They help to fill out the subordinate positions, and form capital material for Roman soldiers or for the populace, and render good assistance in the mechanical labours of the stage. Hence, we see how erroneous it would be to suppose that mere peasants could perform the Passion Play with anything like the fidelity and art of the people of Ober-Ammergau.

The great training school for the Passion Play has been all along the village church, with its purely Catholic ceremonies, its processions, its music and song. The principal festivals, such as the Resurrection and the Ascension, are represented in part dramatically in the Ammergau church. The scenes differ in nothing from the corresponding ones in the Passion Play, except that the figures are not endowed with life. The one is simply a picture or tableau ; the other is a *tableau vivant*. In a hundred ways, indeed, the village church is a preparatory school for the Ammergau drama. The great processions and the harmonious working together of masses of people on the Ammergau stage have excited the admiration even of skilled dramatists. Especially does the opening scene of the play, representing Christ's triumphal entry into Jerusalem, when almost five hundred persons—men, women, and little children—join in the pageant, strike the spectator with amazement. No amount of mere theatrical drilling could have produced such harmony and perfection. In fact, there is only one explanation. All the inhabitants, including the children, have had the opportunity of doing the same thing several times in the year, sometimes within, and sometimes beyond, the limits of the church. Among the principal occasions when such processions take place, we may mention Palm Sunday, Corpus Christi, and a day devoted to thanksgiving, when mass is celebrated at Ettal. The dramatic scene in the Passion Play, of Christ's "Triumphal Entry into Jerusalem," is for the most part a repetition of the church procession on Palm Sunday, even to the singing of the beautiful choral, "All hail! all hail, O David's Son!" The music and singing heard in the Passion Theatre may also be heard in part in the village church, since Dedler, when composing the music for the Passion Play, embodied in his work parts of the masses which he had previously written for Sundays and festivals following the ecclesiastical calendar. Indeed, the village church is the rehearsal theatre for many scenes of the Passion Play, or, better expressed, the people dramatically display on the Passion stage very much of what they have imbibed in the church.

The village school likewise follows the same spirit as the other chief institution of the place, the preceptor acting in subordination to the priest, who is the inspector. One of the necessary qualifications demanded of a school-teacher at Ammergau is that he shall be a musician, and, if possible, a composer. Herr Kirchenhofer, who held that office in 1871, wrote several masses for the village church. The children are very easily taught the elements of music; and they have to learn by heart and to sing passages from the drama which makes the glory of the community. They are also exercised in declaiming parts of the Passion drama. As the children develop, the more musical of the boys gain in time a position in the church orchestra; the girls may become singers in the choir. Later, the more talented may have parts given them for performance in the rehearsal theatre of Ammergau, an institution which comes into requisition during the nine years of interval between the play years, and more especially in the winter preceding the performance of the Passionsspiel. When the public theatre is taken down at the end of the great decennial season, the stage itself is suffered to remain; and preparations are made for a number of other dramatic subjects, partly secular, partly religious, which the villagers perform. These minor plays, exhibited before lesser audiences, were formerly given in a large room, or in a building styled the Rehearsal Theatre, which was sold in 1869. Some of these compositions are by the pen of the Geistlicher Rath Daisenberger, while others are adaptations by him from known German authors. They are acted with great force on the Ammergau boards, and excite the admiration of the whole neighbourhood, visitors coming from some of the more distant towns.

These plays are for the inhabitants instead of pearls and gems. They contemplate them with pride, and store them up in their memory. In particular, they never tire in speaking of Daisenberger's masterpiece, "The Founding of the Monastery of Ettal," with which the reader has already been made acquainted. Of the other original dramatic compositions of this author, which have been brought out on the Ammergau rehearsal stage, we may mention his "Saint Genoveva," "Saint Agatha," "Absalon," "Otto von Wittelsbach at the Veronese Hermitage." The following pieces, of a secular character, he has simply accommodated, or adapted, and admitted to the village boards: "Otto von Wittelsbach," "William Tell," Schleich's comedy, "The Last Witch," and "Burgher and Junker," and the "Karfunkel," by Count Pocci. A "Christmas Play" was performed at Ober-Ammergau some years ago, and attended by hundreds of peasants from the surrounding districts. In all these plays music and song take a prominent place. In ordinary times, especially in winter, there is a performance every week.

Superintending these performances, the Geistlicher-Rath Daisenberger has directed the villagers. For over thirty-five years, from his first coming to the village, he has devoted his whole life to the education of his flock. His whole existence is so completely interwoven with that of his former parishioners, that we must attribute their progress, particularly in the dramatic line, mainly to him. We cannot, therefore, forbear adding a few particulars from the personal history of this remarkable priest. Whoever has seen the aged man of God, with his countenance so expressive of benevolence to us all, whether Protestants or Catholics, will recognize his image in the description which Victor Scheffel makes of a rural priest in the Schwarzwald, though the framework is that of a long past century:—

Plain his life is—where the village
Bound'ry ceases, there the limits
Were to his religious labours.
Way back in the thirty war-years
People thought to do God honour
When they smashed a brother's skull in.
But to him the dark'ning pine-trees
Long ago brought peace of conscience;
Cobwebs hung about his book-case,
And 'twas doubtful if among the
Mass of controversial writings
E'er a one he read or studied !
Altogether, with dogmatics
And the arms of heavy knowledge
Rarely was his conscience troubled ;
But where'er among his flock a
Quarrel still remained unsettled ;
Where the neighbours' rude dissension
And the demon Discord, troubled
Wedded life and love of children,—
Where the day's great want and mis'ry,
Heavily the poor oppressed,

And the needy spirit longed for
Words of hope and consolation,—
There, as messenger of peace, the
Aged pastor's form ne'er failèd.
Had for all, advice and comfort
From his great heart's deepest treasures;
And when in the furthest cottage
One lay on the bed of sickness,
Struggling hard with Death, the bitter ;
Then at midnight, or at any
Hour when his aid was needed—
Mattered not for storm and winter—
Straight he went unto the sick one,
Giving him the parting blessing.
Lonely on through life he wandered
And his richest, great reward was
When a modest child approaching,
Shyly kissed his hand, in greeting :
Often, too, a thankful smile was
Resting on the lips that spake not—
This was for the aged pastor !
Trompeter von Saekkingen.

Daisenberger is the son of a peasant of Oberau, and is now eighty-two years of age. He spent his youth in the monastery of Ettal, with Othmar Weiss, who was his forerunner in the revisal of the Passion Play, accommodating it to modern forms and demands. When he himself saw the acting for the first time, it was in company with his friend Othmar. Even at this early period, his love of music and the religious drama led him to cherish a hope that Ober-Ammergau was the station to which his ecclesiastical superior would one day appoint him. He had the satisfaction of seeing his wishes accomplished. In 1845 the community demanded him by acclamation for their spiritual shepherd. Under his direction, the drama was performed in 1850, when the part of "Christus" was taken by Tobias Flunger. The eminent success which he achieved on that occasion, as Devrient has reported with the warmth of admiration, encouraged him to make still further efforts, in order to elevate the character both of the play and the players. The celebrated actor Lehmann, of Hanover, attended one of the performances of that

THE "GEISTLICHER RATH" DAISENBERGER.
THE REVISER OF THE MODERN VERSION OF THE PASSION PLAY.

year, and was so struck with the way in which the drama had been put on the boards, that he asked to be introduced to the manager. How great was his surprise, when he was brought into the presence of the young priest!

"I undertook the labour," says Daisenberger, "with the best will, for the love of my Divine Redeemer, and with only one object in view, namely, the edification of the Christian world." The author of the "Album of the Passion Play" says: "In addition to his literary efforts Daisenberger undertook the important charge of educating his parishioners up to the level of their dramatic vocation. In his capacity as pastor of the flock, he undertook the direction and arrangement of the dramatic representations, leaving to the churchwarden, George Zwink, the arrangement of the tableaux, and to the schoolmaster, George Schauer, the direction of the music and the rehearsals. In training the community for their arduous and honourable task, the following order was observed. The committee distributed to the players their separate parts. Next came rehearsals for individual actors. In the evening the Pfarrer invited a certain number to his dwelling, where they had first to read their parts in a clear voice, and afterwards to recite them from memory. All the more prominent actors had private lessons, and special attention was paid to those who had to perform the most important functions on the stage. It was scarcely probable that so elaborate a preparation could issue in a failure. The great reputation which Ammergau now enjoys may be said to date from the year 1850. Visitors who witnessed the wonderful success of the Christus of that year, Tobias Flunger, and (as far as the inferior part of Judas permitted) the equally distinguished acting of Gregor Lechner, still speak of what they then beheld with unabated enthusiasm; and the report of Edward Devrient will ever remain a standing monument of that memorable year. Ever since that period the Passion Play has enjoyed uninterrupted prosperity."

A quarter of a century ago the Geistlicher Rath gave a revision of the text of the Passion Play at the instigation of King Ludwig I. For the benefit of his flock he wrote a history of the village. He has published a volume of sermons, entitled "The Fruits of Observations on the Passion." In the midst of his pastoral duties he has written biblical and historical plays and dramas, and "dramatical scenes" from the history of Bavaria. His religious dramatic productions are entitled, "The Death of Abel," "Melchisedek's Sacrifice," "Abraham's Obedience," "Judith," "Naboth." His dramas and dramatic scenes from the history of his Bavarian Fatherland are, "The Founding of the Monastery of Ettal," "Theodolinda," "King Heinrich and Duke Arnuld of Bavaria," "Otto von Wittelsbach at the Veronese Hermitage," "The Bavarians in the Peasants' War," "Luitberge, Duchess of Bavaria." Legendary scenes dramatized are, "St. Agatha" and "St. Genoveva." And what is more striking than all the rest is the fact that the Geistlicher Rath has translated "Antigone" from the Greek, and adapted it to the capacities of the Ammergau players. The addresses of the Choragus in the Passion Play are written by him after the Greek model of strophe and antistrophe. Many of the dramas are written in blank verse.

THE PASSION PLAY.

The selection of the actors for the various *rôles* is a task of great importance, and devolves upon a committee of forty-five householders, together with the priest and the Geistlicher Rath. The election day is in the last week of December of the year before the play; the members first attend divine service. When the committee meets, it is generally found that the principal parts are easily disposed of, and require little discussion. But the minor characters (and it must be remembered that they amount to some hundreds) give rise to many difficulties which must be solved. Sometimes a name is mentioned and finds at once such a general approval that the person proposed is accepted by acclamation. After the decision is made by a majority of voices, there is no further appeal; and it rarely happens that an unfit person is designated. Materials are at hand in abundance. The younger generation is very ambitious to fill the more honourable parts; and the greatest distinction known to an Ammergauer is to have acted the "Christus" in the Passion Play. There were four candidates for the "Christus" of 1870—Josef Maier, Thomas Rendl, Sebastian Deschler and Johann Diemer, all of whom had great natural gifts capacitating them for such an important trust. It had, however, long been an accepted fact in the village that Maier was the one endowed above the others with the requisite qualities. After this point was decided, Rendl was elected as Joseph of Arimathæa, Deschler as Ezekiel, and Diemer took the part of the Choragus.

We have thus gained an insight into the preparations made by the villagers of Ober-Ammergau for their religio-dramatic labours. Before entering upon a description of the eighteen acts or divisions forming the dramatic story of the Passion, it will be of interest to become acquainted with the peculiar structure of the Ammergau Theatre, the origin and destination of the beautiful chorus of Schutzgeister or Guardian Angels, and to understand the relation which singers and players bear to each other and to the audience. The Passion Play being to the villagers an act of religious worship, it is not surprising that they should select Sundays and the great festivals of their church for its performance. The day is announced to the thousands of visitors in a similar manner as are the other great festival days of the church, such as Christmas, Corpus Christi, as well as the King's birthday. Precisely at seven o'clock of the evening preceding the day of performance, the musicians assemble at the extreme end of the village, opposite the house of Tobias Flunger, and, headed by the firemen in uniform, they strike up a lively march, and parade through the principal street of the village, till they reach the meadow on the opposite extremity, where the theatre stands. The music announces the approaching festival day. The visitor to the Passion Play is not permitted to slumber softly on play-day mornings; he is awakened at the early hour of five o'clock by the firing of the village cannon, planted on the meadow at the foot of the Kofel; this early call being intended to enable and to admonish villagers and visitors to attend mass in the church before repairing to the theatre. At seven o'clock the village musicians once more parade through the streets in the same order as on the preceding evening, announcing to the visitors to make their way to the theatre, in order to secure their places, if not already reserved.

The Ammergau Passion Theatre is a structure of very unpretending exterior. It is built entirely of boards, and is partly open to the sky. Considered in its relation to architectural beauty, the interior presents nothing of importance except its simplicity. The auditorium has in width 118 feet, and in depth 168. It occupies an area of nearly 20,000 square feet, and is capable of conveniently seating an audience of from 5,000 to 6,000 persons. The stage has been treated at considerable length by most writers on the Passion Play. Some have found in it traces of the ancient classic theatre of Greece. To others, again, it presents traces and a more perfect form of the mystery theatre of the Middle Ages. The spectator sees, in all, five distinct places of action for the players: first, the proscenium, for the chorus, for processions and the like; second, the central stage, for the *tableaux vivants* and the usual dramatic scenes; third, the palace of Pilate; fourth, the palace of Annas; fifth, the streets of Jerusalem. A vast space is thus placed at the disposal of the manager, not inferior in extent to that in the nine-compartment stage used in the old mystery plays, yet infinitely more artistic in its arrangement. And the most remarkable and beautiful of all the accessories to this really wonderful stage is the natural scenery which delights the eye of the spectator on every side. From the right a well-wooded mountain, and from the left the cross-crowned Kofel gaze down upon the visitors and their artistic entertainers; while the eye, reaching over and beyond the stage, rests upon the charming expanse of flowery meadow belonging to the Ammergau valley, the view extending as far as the white houses of Unter-Ammergau. The grandeur, the freedom, and the sweetness of the landscape impart an air of enchantment to the theatre, enhancing the beauty of the acting, and delightfully filling out all the intervals.

There remain two peculiarities of the Passion Play to which we must devote separate paragraphs—the *tableaux vivants* or prophetic Old Testament types, and the chorus of Schutzgeister. Each of the eighteen acts, containing a series of dramatic scenes complete in itself, is prefaced with one or more of these tableaux, the subject of which is taken from the Old Testament. They stand in the closest connection with the dramatic part of the performance, being so many symbols and prophecies of the scenes from the life of Christ which they are intended to illustrate. The small text-book published by the community of Ober-Ammergau has some very appropriate remarks upon this subject by the Geistlicher Rath Daisenberger. "Our main object," he says, "is to represent the story of Christ's Passion, not by a mere statement of facts, but in its connection with the types and figures and prophecies of the Old Testament. By this manner of treatment an additional, strong light will be cast upon the sacred narrative; and the thoughtful spectator will be able to realize the grand truth that Jesus Christ, the Son of God, made man for our salvation, is the central figure of the inspired volumes. As in the history of the Christian Church the life of the Saviour and all His sacred actions are continually repeated and reproduced, to the extent that (according to Scriptural commentators) He lives over again, suffers and triumphs again in His saints, so it happened before His appearance in the flesh, that the holy patriarchs and other saints of the Old Testament foreshadowed His coming by the events of their history and by their virtuous lives. For He is the eternal Sun of the spiritual world, the Sun of Justice, sending forth His divine rays to illuminate in all directions both His predecessors and successors, no less than His contemporaries. Many of the incidents in the lives of the ancient fathers bear a striking and obvious resemblance to various parts in the life of the Redeemer, and set forth the sufferings, and death, and resurrection so minutely that the Evangelists continually mention some prophecy which was fulfilled. Thus, the heroes of the Scriptures, Adam, the obedient Abraham, Isaac, Joseph, Job, David, Micaiah, Jonas, Daniel, and so many others who laboured and suffered in His Spirit, represent in part, though imperfectly, His life, and through what they accomplished and suffered they became the prophets of that which in Him, the *Urbild*, the primitive type, should take place. In this fundamental thought is the representation of the Passion arranged and performed on the basis of the entire Scriptures."

We now turn our attention to the Chorus of Schutzgeister, or Guardian Angels, this most charming institution of the Ammergau stage. Many writers, following up their general theories upon this subject, recognize in the chorus a simple adaptation of the corresponding part of the classic theatre to modern use. But the assumption is justified only in a slight degree. The chorus consists of eighteen Schutzgeister, with a leader, who is styled the Prologue or Choragus. They have dresses of various colours, over which a white tunic, with a golden fringe, and a coloured mantle are worn. Their appearance on the stage is solemn and majestic. They advance from the recesses on either side of the proscenium, and take up their position across the whole extent of the theatre, forming a slightly concave line. After the chorus has assumed its position, the Choragus gives out in a melodramatic manner the opening address, or prologue, which introduces each act; the tone is immediately taken up by the whole chorus, which continues either in solo, alternately, or in chorus, until the curtain is raised in order to reveal a *tableau vivant*. At this moment the Choragus retires a few steps backward, and forms, with one-half of the band, a division on the left of the stage; while the other half withdraws in like manner to the right. They thus leave the centre of the stage completely free; and the spectators have a full view of the tableau which is thus revealed. A few seconds having been granted for the contemplation of this picture, made more solemn by the musical recitation of the expounders, the curtain falls again, and the two divisions of the chorus coming forward, resume their first position, and present a front to the audience, observing the same grace in all their motions as when they parted. The chanting still continues, and points out the connection between the picture which has just vanished and the dramatic scene which is forthwith to succeed. The singers then make their exit. The task of these Spirit-Singers is resumed in the few following points: they have to prepare the audience for the approaching scenes. While gratifying the ear by delicious harmonies, they explain and interpret the relation which shadow bears to substance, the connection between the type and its fulfilment. And, as their name implies, they must be ever present, as Guardian Spirits, as heavenly monitors, during the entire performance.

The part intrusted to the Chorus of Schutzgeister, and the profound impression their appearance and singing leave upon the spectator, have, perhaps, never been better expressed than in the following "Dialogue with the Chorus of the Passion Play at Ober-Ammergau," the beautiful verses of which are, however, somewhat marred by translation. Their author is a young lady of Augsburg, Fräulein Bertha Thiersch.

Address.
Whence come ye hither, beings fair as day,
   With wondrous voice, and gentle, earnest gaze?
Why in this mountain valley do ye stay?
   And what high theme inspires your songs of praise?

Answer.
Strangers we are! Our joyous youth is fled;
   In distant parts our native valleys lie!
There learnt we song: yet oft we hear it said:
   Good Angels they! sent hither from on high!

Address.
God greet ye all, ye messengers from far!
   I well perceive your glorious mission's aim!
Yea, ye are like to that bright, wondrous star,
   That once gleam'd o'er the hut at Bethlehem!

Answer.
Not ours the fame, not ours the honour vain;
   For what we do—we cannot otherwise!
The Highest God we praise in tuneful strain,
   And He the Son, descended from the skies!

Address.
Mine ear doth list and marvel at your song,
   The heart is moved at your alternate choir:
Ye call up scenes that to the past belong;
   Ye teach us how salvation to acquire!

Answer.
We go lamenting o'er the Saviour's woes;
   We sing His one great sacrificial deed!
On Golgotha we count His parting throes:
   Deeply we feel the human children's need!

Address.
I hear ye sing, with loud exultant breath,
   Praising the vict'ry which for us He gain'd!
He who for us despised not bitter death,
   And for our sins redemption sweet obtain'd!

Answer.
Yea, the Good Master from your view is ta'en,
   No longer doth He in your midst sojourn!
But as He left, so will He come again!
   O sing, rejoicing in His near return!

Address.
Your words of peace and comfort still I hear:
   I see in spirit all those pictures fair!
That God protect and guard this people dear—
   This be the subject of my earnest prayer!

Mrs. Howitt gives her memories of the Schutzgeister in the following beautiful words: "And whilst they sang, our hearts were strangely touched, and our eyes wandered away from those singular peasant-angels and their peasant audience, up to the deep, cloudless sky; we heard the rustle of the trees, and caught glimpses of the mountains, and all seemed a strange, poetical dream."

A single feature more. The villagers consider the play in the light of a precious heirloom, and its performance is a labour of love. In the year 1870 the community refused an offer of a hundred thousand guldens from an enterprising German, who wished to farm the receipts for that year. In 1871 they again refused very tempting offers, when they were invited to perform in America and England; and in 1872 they vanquished another temptation. A sum of sixty thousand florins was offered to the community, on the condition that some of its members would perform the Passion Play in Vienna, during the Exposition of 1873, which they likewise refused. The community is on the whole a moderate gainer. The individuals lose in neglected work more than they are paid for their *rôles*. A good portion of the receipts is applied to municipal purposes. In the distribution of the honorarium among the players, it is customary to regulate the amounts according to the number of words which they have to recite, and according to the prominence of the character delineated. In 1871 no actor received more than two hundred florins, with the exception of Joseph Maier, for his delineation of Christ, and he surpassed this sum only by twenty florins. In 1870 his remuneration consisted in the sum of one hundred and sixty florins, the same amount which his predecessor of 1860, Rupus Schauer, had received. Tobias Flunger received for the same part in 1850 a sum of but sixty florins, or five pounds sterling! These good people assuredly deserve all they can earn in the Passion year, which comes only once in every decade; for wood-carving is very meagrely paid. Even Joseph Maier, the delineator of Christ, who is a skilful workman, does not earn over eight florins per week in ordinary times; and Flunger (Pilate), with his whole family of five or six working members, scarcely double that amount! True, the wants of the people are easily satisfied, and their plot of meadow and their fruit gardens help to make life more comfortable than it seems at the first glance.

Thus, with a knowledge of the history of the village of Ober-Ammergau, the character of the inhabitants, and the influences under which they live, the reader will be the better able to appreciate the Passion Play, and to understand the "secret spell that enabled the wood-carvers of a village in the highlands of Bavaria to attract multitudes of men and women, whom the highest efforts of histrionic art would fail to tempt fifty miles from their own firesides at home." The people of Ammergau are not remarkable either for extraordinary genius or for eminent sanctity, as the vulgar notion supposes; but they enjoy the advantage of having been instructed by trials of various kinds; and the hardships entailed by the mountain valley in which they live have contributed to bring out all their faculties, while their dramatic talent has been developed by a happy blending of local and religious influences, disseminated primarily by the church and its teachers.

THE PASSION THEATRE AND THE "KOFEL."

THE PASSION PLAY.

PART I.—FROM CHRIST'S TRIUMPHAL ENTRY INTO JERUSALEM TO THE BETRAYAL IN GETHSEMANE.

THE PROLOGUE.

TABLEAU I. The Fall: Adam and Eve expelled from Eden.
TABLEAU II. The Redemption: The Adoration of the Cross.

THE Passion Play has a double prelude, one of Prayer and one of Nature. Precisely at eight o'clock the booming of cannon planted beneath the peak of the Kofel announces that the drama is about to be commenced. If the curtain of the central stage were removed while the musical overture is being played, so as to at once reveal what is only to be gradually unfolded, the heart of many indifferent spectators would be filled with surprise. In the principal scene of the future labours of the players assemble all the members of the community who are to take an active part in the performances, upwards of five hundred in number, together with their pastor, and there engage in silent prayer. That is the unseen prelude to the Passion Play. There is also the prelude of Nature. The eye, wandering far beyond the limits of the stage, dwells upon the green sun-bathed landscape of the valley. To the right and left the gaze rests on mountains fringed with firs, and, more prominent than all, on the high-peaked Kofel, with its high cross gilded by the morning's rays. The ear of the visitor is captivated by soft, thrilling melodies, as the lark soars from her nest among the meadow grass beyond, and pours out her morning hymn to the Creator. From the distant hills the tinkling of the cow-bells comes faintly to the ear. Nature and Art unite in preparing the mind for the grand scene of Christ's triumphal entry into Jerusalem. A wonderful prelude, which has inspired in an English poet the following beautiful lines:—

How clearly on my inner sense are borne	The birds that o'er us from the upper day
The fair, fresh beauty of the mountain morn,	Threw flitting shade, and went their airy way,—
And cries of flocks afar, and mixed with these	The bright-robed chorus and the silent throng,
The green delightful tumult of the trees.	And that first burst and sanctity of song!

The Chorus of Schutzgeister appears upon the stage. They stand before the audience with hands folded across the breast, in the attitude of prayerful repose. The Choragus opens the Play by explaining the main object of the whole performance: how the fallen human race became reconciled to God through the blood of His only-begotten Son. This main object, the whole extent and scope of the Passion Play, is to be exhibited in two tableaux, which the Choragus introduces in a brief prologue. The first type represents the expulsion of Adam and Eve from Eden—symbolical of the Fall; the second, the Adoration of the Cross—typical of Redemption. We have in these two tableaux a wonderful symbolism: the Tree of Death with the forbidden fruit, whose mortal taste brought sin and sorrow into the world: the Tree of Life, or the Cross, symbolical of hope and refuge for sinful and repentant humanity. The first verse of the intoned prologue falls with powerful intensity on the ear:—

Wirf zum heiligen Staunen dich nieder,	O, human race! by sin and shame laid low,
Von Gottes Fluch gebeugtes Geschlecht!	Adore thy God: bend down and kiss the dust!
Friede dirr—aus Sion Gnade wieder!	Peace then shall come, and grace from Zion flow:
Nicht ewig zürnt Er,	Not ever spurns He
Der Beleidigte—ist sein Zürnen gleich gerecht.	The Offended One: although His wrath is just!
"Ich will"—so spricht der Herr—	"I will," the Lord doth say,
"Den Tod des Sünders nicht—vergeben	"Not that the sinner die—forgive
Will ich ihm—er soll leben!	Will I his guilt, and he shall live!
Versöhnen wird ihn selbst meines Sohnes Blut, versöhnen!"	My Son's own blood shall now atone for him!"
Preis, Anbetung, Freudenthränen, Ewiger Dir!	Praise, worship, tears of joy to Thee, Eternal One!

FIRST TABLEAU.—After the Choragus has finished, the Chorus divides and retires to the extremities of the central stage. The first typical picture is then revealed. Adam and Eve driven out of the Garden of Eden by the angel with the flaming sword, flee from the threatened punishment. Paradise is in the background, and in the centre is seen the tree of life, laden with luscious fruit, while from its branches the tempter, in the form of a serpent, is seen. While the tableau is exposed to the gaze of the spectators, the Choragus gives in song the story of its significance :—

Die Menschheit ist verbannt aus Edens Au'n Von Sünd' umnachtet und von Todes-Grau'n. Ihr ist zum Lebensbaum—der Eingang ach! versperrt. Es drohet in des Cherubs Hand das Flammenschwert.	From Eden and its tree of knowledge bann'd, See our first parents, sin-benighted, stand! God, through the cherub, doth His wrath proclaim, And guards the entrance with a sword of flame!
Doch von Ferne, von Calvarias Höhen Leuchtet durch die Nacht ein Morgenglüh'n; Aus des Kreuzbaumes Zweigen wehen Friedenslüfte durch die Welten hin.	But in the distance, from 'mid Calvary's throes, Through the dark night the glow of morn appears. See, from the branches of the Cross there flows Sweet, balmy peace to all created spheres!
Gott! Erbarmer! Sünder zu begnaden, Die verachtet schändlich Dein Gebot, Gibst Du, von dem Fluche zu entladen, Deinen Eingebornen in den Tod.	O, God of mercy, full of wondrous love, Those Thou forgiv'st who spurn Thy high decree! Thy first-born Son Thou sendest from above To die, that sinners may find grace with Thee!

SECOND TABLEAU.—The curtain falls after the Choragus has sung the first stanza. When the Schutzgeister have taken up their positions across the entire extent of the stage, the leader announces the message of salvation. Then the Chorus retires and the second tableau, the Adoration of the Cross, is revealed. Before a large cross, planted on a rock (symbolical of Christianity), a number of heavenly genii (little children of the village clad in garments of white and mantles of bright colours) stand or kneel in the attitude of worship. The tableau, so beautiful in itself, is executed with marvellous art by these infant dramatists. The angelic forms and their tiny wards are silent, but the feelings by which they are animated, and the prayer of which their hearts are full, find utterance in the words of the Schutzgeister, who fall upon their knees and chant the following hymn :—

Ew'ger! höre deiner Kinder Stammeln! Weil ein Kind ja nichts als stammeln kann; Die beim groszen Opfer sich versammeln, Beten Dich voll heil'ger Ehrfurcht an.	Eternal God, O hear Thy children's prayer, Though children-like we pray with faltering tone; Those who to see the Sacrifice repair, Bow low in faith and worship at Thy throne!
Folget dem Versöhner nun zur Seite, Bis er seinen rauhen Dornenpfad Durchgelaufen, und im heissen Streite Blutend für uns ausgekämpfet hat.	Oh! follow close by the Redeemer's side, The while He, patient, treads the thorny path; Nor leave Him while He struggles with the tide, Until for you the victory He hath.

In this brief prologue, in the plastic tableaux, and the songs of the Chorus, are embodied the general outline of the drama and the whole scope of the drama of redemption.

ACT I.—CHRIST'S ENTRY INTO JERUSALEM.

THE Chorus has scarcely disappeared when the first dramatic act of the Passion Play commences. From the distance, beyond the city as it were, sounds of rejoicing, of glad shouting and singing, are heard. The audience must, in this case, leave imagination to supply the scenery. Down the slope of Olivet comes the Messianic procession, and one hears the singing and rejoicing of the crowds of Passover pilgrims and the people of Jerusalem who welcome Jesus to the Holy City. From the side streets bands of Hebrew children, led by their parents or teachers, come forth to join the throng that has already collected about Christ. In the midst of the crowd we distinguish Christ Himself, seated upon the ass, and His disciples following. The procession passes from the central stage to the street leading into Jerusalem, and then through the gateway at the right of the stage into the sunshine of the broad proscenium (which represents Jerusalem). There are fully five hundred persons before Him. The children, boys and girls, wave their palm branches and sing with full hearts their Hosannas, and men and women of all ages, clad in picturesque costumes, join in the exultant crowd. The person of the Saviour, surrounded by His disciples and the welcoming multitude, forms the central figure of the scene. He remains seated upon the ass, and raises His hands as if to bless or teach the people, though His words are lost in the strains of the beautiful Hosanna-chorus, sung by hundreds of voices:—

Heil Dir! Heil Dir! O Davids Sohn!
Heil Dir! Heil Dir! der Väter Thron
        Gebühret Dir.
Der in des Höchsten Namen kömmt,
Dem Israel entgegenströmt,
        Dich preisen wir.

Hosanna! der im Himmel wohnet,
Der sende alle Huld auf Dich.
Hosanna! der dort oben thronet,
Erhalte uns Dich ewiglich.
        Heil Dir, &c.

Gesegnet sei, das neu auflebet,
Des Vaters David Volk und Reich!
Ihr Völker segnet, preiset, hebet
Den Sohn empor, dem Vater gleich.
        Heil Dir, &c.

Hosanna unserm Königssohne!
Ertöne durch die Lüfte weit!
Hosanna! auf des Vaters Throne
Regiere er voll Herrlichkeit!
        Heil Dir, &c.

All hail! all hail! O David's Son!
All hail! all hail! Thy Father's throne
        Belongs to Thee!
Who cometh in the name most high,
Whom Israel's children glorify,
        We praise but Thee!

Hosanna! He that dwells above,
Send down from heaven all grace to Thee:
Hosanna! may the God of love
Keep us as Thine eternally!
        All hail, &c.

O blissful day that shall restore
Our father David's throne and race!
Ye peoples come, and God adore,
Who gives us of His constant grace!
        All hail, &c.

Hosanna! to our royal Son!
On every breeze send forth the strain!
Hosanna! on His Father's throne
In majesty He aye will reign!
        All hail! All hail!

The chief object of attraction, the figure of Christ, is now before every eye. He has reached the centre of the proscenium, and descends with grace-

ACT I.—CHRIST'S ENTRY INTO JERUSALEM.

ful ease from the animal on which He has been sitting. Of tall stature and noble bearing, with long flowing hair of jet black, falling luxuriantly over his shoulders, the actor who represents the Saviour appears. Of the scene a writer said in 1871: "No painting ever brought to the mind so complete a realization of our ideal as this dramatic delineator, whose life has been one of years of preparation for his task. No spectator could have gazed upon the Saviour, although in the drama, for the first time and remain untouched by the solemnity and grandeur of the scene." The great German dramatist Edward Devrient, who wrote an interesting book on the Passion Play of 1850, when Tobias Flunger was the delineator of the character of Christ, said: "The scene was noble and affecting. A most wonderful impression was made when the Saviour Himself, with whose form our imagination had been busied ever since the days of childhood, seemed actually to stand bodily before us, moving, and exercising an indescribable authority. The figure was full of heavenly mildness and majesty. The appearance and the movements were such as to make us imagine that some mediæval painting had been endowed with life." Joseph Maier has a grander presence than either of his predecessors; although Flunger's personification seems to have been milder and sweeter. While the people gather about the Saviour, a new scene is revealed.

THE TEMPLE SCENE.—A number of high-priests and individuals belonging to the Pharisees, attracted by the noise and the general commotion, enter the proscenium by the opposite gateway, that is, as if coming from within Jerusalem. The Saviour, having descended from the ass, addresses His disciples in words which give full intimation of His approaching sufferings and death. "The hour is come that the Son of man should be glorified. Verily, verily, I say unto you, except a corn of wheat fall into the ground and die, it abideth alone: but if it die, it bringeth forth much fruit." (John xii. 23, 24.) Suddenly a calm is perceived spreading over the multitude. The Hosannas have subsided, and Christ approaches the centre of the proscenium, when, the curtain of the central stage being raised, the scene described in Mark xi. 15 appears in all its remarkable interest before the spectators. "Jesus went into the Temple, and began to cast out them that bought and sold in the Temple, and overthrew the tables of the money-changers, and the seats of them that sold doves." With a feeling of deep sadness and consternation the Lord beholds the signs of profanation in His Father's house, near the stately columns of whose entrance the traders have set up their tables. At this sight the Saviour, folding His hands as if to offer a silent prayer, advances with a dignified air towards the profaners and, in a tone of mingled grief and indignation, exclaims: "What is this I see? Is this the house of God, or is it a market-place! Must the strangers who come from the lands of the Heathen to adore Jehovah perform their devotions among the throng of money-changers? And ye priests, guardians of the Sanctuary, can you look on this abomination and suffer it to continue? Woe to this venal race of hirelings! He who searches the heart knows wherefore ye tolerate and further such disorder!" "Who is this man?" asks one of the traders. The people, gazing with anxiety upon the scene, exclaim: "It is the great prophet from Nazareth, in Galilee!" Christ advances with conscious dignity toward the buyers and sellers, and says: "Away from this place, children of Mammon! I command you to depart. Take what is yours, and leave the sacred place!"

Whilst uttering these words the Lord takes from one of the booths a number of cords used for the tethering of lambs brought for sacrifice, and plaits them into a scourge with His own hands. He then advances to where the traffic is most vigorous and noisy, and, to the great consternation of the traders, overturns their seats and tables. Jars are dashed to the ground and broken; the doves are released from their cages and fly in haste to their cotes in the city (village); and the money-changers, unable to rescue all their effects, gather the coins which lie scattered on the ground. During the whole of this energetic display of zeal and authority the Saviour never loses His dignified composure. A scene of still greater confusion follows. The priesthood, led by Caiaphas and Annas, appear in a manner which strikingly contrasts with the majesty, sanctity, and just indignation of the Redeemer, whom they refuse to recognize. Sadoc, one of the Council, addresses Christ: "By what authority dost thou this?" The high-priests charge Christ with rebelling against the religion of Moses and the prophets, and seek thus to win the people to them, crying: "Revenge! revenge! With us, ye that belong to Moses! Moses is our prophet!" Their cry is heartily endorsed by the disturbed buyers and sellers; it is seen how easily the multitude becomes impressed by the addresses of the high-priests and Pharisees, especially of Caiaphas. While the enraged Pharisees and merchants retire, plotting against the Saviour, the latter takes dignified leave of the people, and returns with His disciples to Bethany.

In this act of the Passion Play we see the germ of the conspiracy that leads to the final catastrophe. Edward Devrient said of the scene (in 1850): "One thing has become with me a settled conviction. If I had entertained a doubt as to the propriety of representing sacred subjects upon the stage, all such hesitation would vanish from this hour. Here can be nothing said of a profanation of our ideal of the Redeemer. On the contrary, the picture which I had hitherto endeavoured to represent to my mental vision of the Son of God taking a visible form and acting His part on the theatre of the world, in the midst of His friends and opponents,—this picture reappeared at Ammergau; and, deprived of its dream-like vagueness, assumed all the vigour of life and reality. I beheld for the first time the God-Man as a pilgrim on the earth. In His triumphal entry into Jerusalem, when the multitude hailed Him with shouts of Hosanna, I read on His brow that His thoughts were turned far from the present scene of jubilation in order to contemplate the completion of His sacrifice on Calvary. Knowing that the torments and the ignominy of the Cross were a necessary part of His heavenly Father's scheme of salvation, He kept aloof from the sentiments of the excited multitude, and was no more allured by their songs of triumph than He was afterwards daunted by their persecution, abuse, and blasphemy. He knew that He must be betrayed, denied, abandoned by all, mocked, scourged,

JOSEPH MAIER,
THE DELINEATOR OF "CHRIST" IN 1870, 1871, AND IN 1880.

ACT II.—THE HIGH COUNCIL.

crowned with thorns and crucified. It was by means of the village tragedy that I confronted these great truths of revelation. I then felt how deep is the wound which has been inflicted by humanity against its Ideal. The tragedy was more powerful than word or painting."

ACT II.—THE HIGH COUNCIL.

TABLEAU. The sons of Jacob conspire against their brother Joseph.—Gen. xxxvii. 18.

THE conspiracy, which is delineated in the first act, is brought to maturity in the second, in the conclave of the priests and scribes. The point of connection between the two is supplied both by the Choragus and the Chorus. The part of the former is to deliver to the audience a suitable address, in the melodramatic style,—an expository survey of the events which have already transpired, together with intelligent hints concerning what is yet to come. The Chorus then sings of the connection of the tableaux with the dramatic scenes and their teachings, thus drawing the past and the future nearer to each other. The addresses with which the Choragus opens every succeeding act are the composition of the Geistlicher Rath Daisenberger. They are written in the form of the ancient strophe and antistrophe, with the difference that, whilst in the Greek theatre they were spoken by different members of the chorus, they are delivered in the Passion Play by the Choragus alone:—

"*All hail! Welcome to the band of brothers whom love divine hath here assembled; who wish to share the sorrows of their Saviour, and to follow Him, step by step, on the way of His sufferings—to the cross and to the sepulchre. All who have come hither from far and near, feel themselves united in brotherly love, as the disciples of the One who died for us all, and who, full of mercy and compassion, gave Himself up to the bitter death for us. Let our gaze and heart, then, be directed towards Him in harmonious thankfulness. Behold! He feeleth the approach of the hour of tribulation. He is ready to drink of the cup of sorrow. For now the serpent-brood of the envious have formed a plot with avarice to bring Him speedily to ruin. That bitter form of malice which once inspired the brothers of Joseph with murderous desires, so that they shamelessly complotted in fanatical wickedness to put the innocent to death, is urging on the fallen priestly race to remove the Herald of truth from the number of the living.*"

At the end of this address the orchestra strikes up an appropriate melody, and a tableau, typical of the mystery, is revealed, the Choragus and his band continuing their melodious recitation and explanations :—

Ha! sind sie fort die losen Bösewichte—	Ah! are they gone, the ruthless sons of spite?
Entlarvt die scheussliche Gestalt im vollen Lichte—	Their sordid forms and aims are brought to light!
Die Tugendlappe von dem Sünderrock gerissen—	From sin's 'vile garb the shreds of grace are torn,
Gegeisselt von dem nagenden Gewissen.	

"Auf lasset uns"—so schrei'n sie wild—	By keen remorse the face is sear'd and worn!
"auf Rache sinnen,	"Up, let us think on vengeance!" wild they cry,
Den längst entworfenen Plan beginnen!"	"The plot long laid commence: the man shall die!"
Der Heuchler Plan malt uns das graue Alterthum,	By envy's goad urged on, and vengeful ire,
Wie Jakobs Söhne gegen Joseph sich verschwören,	Lo! 'gainst their brother, Jacob's sons conspire;
So werdet ihr von dieser Natterbrut	So now, a fallen race, a hideous brood,
Bald über Jesus "Tod und Blut"	Thirst with a tiger's rage for Jesus' blood!
Voll Tigerrache rufen hören.	

FIRST TABLEAU.—While the Chorus divides the curtain is raised, and the tableau or prophetic picture is revealed. The history itself is recorded in Genesis xxxvii. The scene is the plain of Dothan, on which Joseph found his brethren and their flocks, and where the sequel of the biblical narrative took place. In the foreground we see the brethren of Joseph, some leaning upon their shepherd's staves, others seated on the ground. Their garments are of various colours, and of a coarse texture. Joseph is more in the background. He wears the bright coat which his father gave him as a sign of distinction, and which caused him so much persecution. The sons of Jacob have already taken their resolution. Joseph is to be cast into a well, against the walls of which one of the sturdy figures of this group is leaning. The Chorus sings in solo and duet, alternately, and united:—

Sehet dort, der Träumer kömmt	"See, the dreamer cometh nigh!
Er will, schrei'n sie unverschämt,	As a king," enraged they cry,
Als ein König uns regieren.	"Us to govern, he presumeth!
Fort mit diesem Schwärmer, fort!	This impostor we'll expel!
Ha! in der Cisterne dort	Let him in this empty well
Mag er seinen Plan ausführen.	Wear the robes he now assumeth!"
So nach des Gerechten Blut	Thus, too, is the viper's brood
Dürstet jene Natterbrut.	Thirsting for the righteous blood.
Er ist, schrei'n sie, uns entgegen:	"Honour we must save," they cry,
Unsre Ehre liegt daran—	"Him they seek, from us they fly!
Alles ist ihm zugethan—	What we love He e'er opposeth,
Wandelt nicht nach unsern Wegen.	And His life our life discloseth!"
Kommet, lasset uns ihn tödten!	"Come, and if we can decoy Him—
Niemand kann und mag ihn retten.	Hasten, seize Him, and destroy Him!
Laszt uns fest darauf besteh'n!	Onward push the plans we cherish—
Fort! er soll zu Grunde geh'n.	Now away, He sure must perish!"
Gott vertilge diese Frevler-Rotte,	Destroy, O God, these impious bands,
Die sich wider Dich empört.	Who scorn Thy name, their vices boast,
Und den Mörderbund zum Spotte	Thy Son expose to murderers' hands;
Deines Eingebornen schwört.	Exterminate the recreant host.
Lasse Deiner Allmacht Donner brüllen,	O let Thy mighty thunders peal
Deine Rechte Blitze glüh'n,	And lightning, fraught with ruin, flash;
Dasz sie Deiner Rache Stärke fühlen,	Let all Thy terrors sinners feel;
Schmett're in den Staub sie hin.	Their bones to dust in vengeance dash!

The two last stanzas give vent to such an impetuous zeal, and are of

ACT II.—THE HIGH COUNCIL.

such a vehement character, that some counterbalancing influence was felt to be wanting. Accordingly the following strains, breathing reconciliation, are commended by the soothing accents of two female voices, breaking in upon the Chorus. The last stanza is sung by the entire Chorus:—

Aber, nein, er kam nicht zum Verderben	No, you know not God's most secret plan!
Von des Vaters Herrlichkeit;	When the Son His Father's glory left,
Alle Sünder sollen durch ihn erben	Grace He brought, and bliss to sinful man,
Gnade, Huld und Seligkeit.	Again enriching him, of all his gifts bereft!
Voll der Demuth beten dann	Meek and humble, full of awe,
Deiner Liebe groszen Plan,	We, Thy children, evermore,
Gott! wir, Deine Kinder, an.	Thy holy will and all Thy ways adore.

THE HIGH COUNCIL.—The Chorus retires from the proscenium. The rising curtain reveals within the central stage the dramatic scene typically foreshadowed by the conspiracy of Dothan. The scene is the Jewish Sanhedrim, the assembly of the high-priests of the Synagogue, who purpose discussing what measures shall be taken against the Galilean. The priests composing the assembly are seated on benches about the room; Caiaphas and Annas presiding during the debates. The breast of the former is graced with the most sublime of all Jewish decorations, namely, the shield or breastplate containing twelve precious stones, with the names of the twelve tribes of Israel. Annas, not being actually in supreme power, does not wear the breastplate; his costume is entirely of white. The Sanhedrim does not lose much time before commencing the earnest business that has called the members together. Caiaphas, the violent, irritable, despotic high-priest (admirably represented by Johann Lang), is the first to rise. With a penetrating, threatening voice, he opens the discussion. " Venerable assembly of priests, teachers, and fathers of the people!" he exclaims. "Our religion, our laws, are in danger of being cast down. Shall we again celebrate the Easter festival? Is not the Galilean prince in Jerusalem? Did He not drive out the buyers and sellers from the Temple, with the scourge? He has also attacked Moses and the prophets! How long shall we dally? Who shall restrain the people from being led away? It is fearful! Have you not seen how He entered our city in triumph? Shall we wait here until the last shadow of our power is gone? It is better that *one* die." The assembly cry out as with one voice, "We, too, declare for His death!" The aged Annas rises from his seat, and speaks with passion, "By my grey hairs I swear not to rest until the inheritance of our religion is secured by His death." The question arises, how can they get Christ into their power, since He has so many followers among the people. Money and promises appear to them the most appropriate means; and the buyers and sellers of the Temple the ready tools for their revenge. Two delegates are then sent to fetch the usurers to the assembly, and the latter shortly afterwards appear. They say that they do not fear the people, the adherents of Jesus, and cry, "Did not the High Council give us permission to buy and sell within the Temple? And has not the Galilean driven us therefrom? Yes, with a scourge did He drive us out! He must suffer for it with His blood.

Revenge! Revenge!" They then receive the commission from the Sanhedrim to find out Christ's place of sojourn; and while they are discussing further the plan of revenge, one among them says that he knows one of the disciples of Christ, whom he thinks capable of betraying his Master. The Sanhedrim is closed by Annas rising, and addressing the members in the following words: "Fathers and friends! In my old days I could almost leap for joy! I feel anew my heart warmed through. As from a sweet slumber I awake. Let us go, and do what we have determined upon. Praised be our fathers, Moses, Isaac, and Jacob." Devrient said that at this point he thought he could not better designate the method of representation than by saying it was to him as if pictures of mediæval painters had become endowed with life.

ACT III.—CHRIST'S DEPARTURE FROM BETHANY.

TABLEAU I. Young Tobias taking leave of his parents.—Tobias v. 32.
TABLEAU II. The Lamenting Bride of the Canticles.—Song of Solomon vi.

AFTER the last visit to Jerusalem, where the enemies of Christ had become stronger and bolder, He continued His practice of leaving the tumultuous city at sunset, and going with His disciples to Bethany, where He stayed until the morning, and then returned to Jerusalem. Bethany was to the Lord a beloved sojourn. It was not only the home of Simon the leper, but also of Lazarus, whom He had raised from the dead, and of his two sisters Mary and Martha: It is to be observed that Mary was, in all probability, the same person as Mary Magdalene, and the Ammergau dramatists consider her as such, though the point is disputed by several noted critics. The scene of Christ's taking leave of His mother is laid in Bethany. The two principal scenes connected therewith, the anointing of the Saviour's feet by Mary Magdalene, and the parting from His mother, are indicated and introduced by two tableaux. The one represents young Tobias about to depart from his parents; the other, the Lamenting Bride of the Canticles. The connection between these Old Testament types and the dramatic incidents is made sufficiently conspicuous by the explanatory address of the Choragus:—

"*He who, with clear gaze, can penetrate the veil of the future already sees the storm that is gathering, and which will soon pour its vengeance upon His head. During the last brief hours, whilst tarrying amid His friends, He intimates to them His departure in words which painfully wound the spirit of His beloved mother. See how sorrowful is the mother of Tobias as she gazes on the departing son so dear to her heart. Her pain finds relief in streaming tears. Even so the mother of Jesus sighs and weeps when she beholds her divine Son going with resolute step to His fate, resolved on freeing humanity of sin by His death. See the spouse in the Song of Solomon, how she laments because the Bridegroom has disappeared! How she weeps, and searches, and allows herself no repose until she has again found the object of her affections. The pain in the soul of Mary is more tranquil. Her heart is,*

ACT III.—CHRIST'S DEPARTURE FROM BETHANY.

indeed, pierced as with a sword, but she bears the wound with pious resignation, and never loses confidence in God."

The musical performance opens with a single female voice; and presently the Chorus joins in, and introduces the first tableau with a pathetic melody, accompanying these words:—

Ach, sie kommt die Scheidestunde,	The parting hour is now approaching,
Und sie schlägt die tiefste Wunde,	The sea of bitterness encroaching,
O, Maria, in dein Herz.	O, sweet Mary, on thy heart!
Ach, dein Sohn muss dich verlassen,	Alas, thy Son, He now must leave thee,
Um am Kreuze zu erblassen!	On the Cross to die, bereave thee!
Wer ermiszt den Mutterschmerz?	Who can heal the mother's smart?

FIRST TABLEAU.—After the chanting of these words the Chorus divides and retires, in order to direct the gaze of the audience upon the tableau of young Tobias leaving his parental home. The aged father sends his boy to a distant city; but the latter, not knowing which road to take, goes out to seek some one who may accompany him as a guide. He finds the angel Raphael standing at the door, with staff in hand, and with provisions; in a word, quite ready for the journey. The features of young Tobias are overcast with a shade of melancholy, occasioned by the thought of parting from his beloved parents. Full of confidence, however, he gives his right hand to the angel. In the foreground is seen the dog mentioned in the biblical narrative as having accompanied Tobias in his wanderings. The picture is revealed whilst the first two stanzas of the following melody are being sung by the Chorus:—

Freunde, welch' ein herber Schmerz	O, friends, see what a fearful pain
Folterte das Mutterherz,	The mother's heart doth here contain
Als Tobias an der Hand	When, by the father's high command,
Raphaels in fremdes Land	Her son leaves for a foreign land—
Auf Befehl des Vaters eilte!	An angel as his guide.
Unter tausend Weh' und Ach	She grieves; and, 'mid her tears and sighs,
Ruft sie dem Geliebten nach:	How often to her boy she cries,
Komme, ach, verweile nicht,	"My heart's sole trust, and light and song!
Meines Herzens Trost und Licht!	My boy! nor tarry thou so long
Komme, komme bald zurücke!	From thy sad mother's side."
Ach, Tobias! Theuerster!	And, mother-like, her soul oppress'd,
Eil' in meine Arme her,	She prays that all his ways be bless'd;
Liebster Sohn! an dir allein	"Dear boy," she cries, "alone in thee
Wird mein Herz sich wieder freu'n,	Can my poor heart rejoicèd be—
Freuen sich der schönsten Freude.	In thee, my only pride!"
Trostlos jammert sie nun so,	Thus comfortless, lamenting, sad,
Nimmer ihres Lebens froh,	And never in her life long glad,
Bis ein sel'ger Augenblick	Until an hour of blissful joy
In den Mutterschooss zurück	Brings back once more the long-lost boy
Den geliebten Sohn wird führen.	Unto the mother's side.

SECOND TABLEAU.—The second tableau, the Lamenting Bride of the Canticles, is, like the first, intended to prepare the audience for the scene which succeeds—the departure of Christ from Bethany and His taking leave of Mary. The scene is laid in a luxuriant flower-garden. The sorrowing Bride, clad in snow-white, is surrounded by her bridesmaids chosen from among the daughters of Jerusalem. They look with tender sympathy upon their distressed mistress, and would fain comfort her with singing and sweet strains from their harps and cymbals. This tableau has frequently been condemned as the least appropriate symbolic picture of the play, but the idea embodied in it is peculiarly delicate. One of the most usual comparisons adopted in Scripture to set forth the union of Christ and the Church is that of a marriage, in which Christ is represented as the bridegroom and the Church as a bride. The accompanying solo is rendered by the first female voice of the Chorus. It is intended to express the lament of the Bride, sung to the daughters of Jerusalem. The following is a rendering of the words:—

THE BRIDE'S LAMENT.

Wo ist er hin? Wo ist er hin	Oh! where doth my Beloved stay?
Der Schöne aller Schönen?	Of mortals he the fairest!
Mein Auge weinet, ach! um ihn	For him I weep my life away!
Der Liebe heisse Thränen.	What sorrow, heart, thou bearest!
Ach, komme doch! ach, komme doch!	Oh, come to me! oh, come to me!
Sieh diese Thränen fliessen:	Oh, see these hot tears flowing!
Geliebter! wie? Du zögerst noch	Beloved! what? why tarryest thou
Dich an mein Herz zu schliessen?	To clasp my heart o'erflowing?
Mein Auge forschet überall	Mine eye is ever seeking thee,
Nach Dir auf allen Wegen:	In all the world surrounding;
Und mit der Sonne erstem Strahl	And with the sun's first beam of light
Eilt Dir mein Herz entgegen.	My heart to thee is bounding.

THE CHORUS, COMFORTING THE BRIDE.

Geliebter! ach! was fühle ich?	Beloved, ah, what do I feel?
Wie ist mein Herz beklommen!	My heart is fill'd with sorrow!
Geliebte Freundin! tröste Dich;	Beloved maid, be comforted
Dein Freund wird wieder kommen.	For meeting comes a-morrow!
O harre Freundin! bald kommt er,	Oh, maiden, wait; he soon will come
Schlingt sich an Deine Seite;	And clasp thy true heart beating;
Dann trübet keine Wolke mehr	Then troubles ne'er a dark cloud more
Des Wiedersehens Freude.	The joy of lovers' meeting!

UNITING WITH THE CHORUS, THE BRIDE ANSWERS:

O komm' in meine Arme her,	Oh, come into my arms; Oh, come!
Schling Dich an meine Seite;	Oh, clasp my heart in sweet communion
Und keine Wolke trübe mehr	No dark cloud, then, shall cast its gloom
Des Wiedersehens Freude.	Upon our glad, our last reunion!

THE ANOINTMENT.—Christ appears with His disciples in the streets of Bethany. The Lord tells His followers that the hour of parting has come. But beyond death He promises to see them again. Christ's words induce the good-hearted Peter to say, "Master, this idea of parting will not enter my head at all!" All the disciples are deeply sorrowful at Christ's words; only Judas shows anxiety for his future material life. Christ perceives this disciple's thoughts, and says, "Judas, do not be more troubled than is necessary;" and to the others He says, "My good disciples, your thoughts are much too human; be comforted and follow me." All this is spoken on the way. Soon the house of Simon is reached; some of the family appear to in-

ACT III.—CHRIST'S DEPARTURE FROM BETHANY.

vite Jesus to enter; and He follows the invitation. The scene then changes into a banquet room; Christ and His disciples take places at the table, and Martha waits upon the guests. Jesus takes a place to the left of the table; and while He addresses His disciples, Magdalena with her costly ointment appears, casts herself at the Saviour's feet, and anoints them, full of penitence and love. While engaged in anointing Christ's feet, the disciples gather around in astonishment, while Judas points excitedly to the event. Görres has well remarked on this scene: "Here come two opposite sensations to direct prominence. The good and the evil angels stand opposed: to the right kneels penitent Love at the feet of her good Saviour, who, forgiving, permits the anointment; to the left stands Envy, who, selfish and cold, calculates the material value of the offering, and would fain make it appear before the world that his selfishness is sympathy and love for the poor." "What a costly ointment!" Judas says; "why does he not hinder the foolish woman? What a waste of money! How many poor people could have been supported from it. Three hundred pence would certainly have been got for it." Magdalena, in her deep pain and penitence, can only utter the pleading words, "Rabbi! Rabbi!" And Jesus says: "Let her alone; why trouble ye her? She hath wrought a good work on Me.... Verily I say unto you, Wheresoever this gospel shall be preached throughout the whole world, this also that she hath done shall be spoken of for a memorial of her." Finally Christ rises, and thanks Simon for his hospitality. The good family appear sad at Christ's departure, when Jesus comforts them by giving them hopes that they shall soon meet again. He tells the disciples to follow Him. "Whither?" they ask. "Let us not go to Jerusalem!" Jesus answers, "Follow me: the rest ye shall see."

THE PARTING AT BETHANY.—"Come, then," adds Christ, and leads the way; Mary Magdalene and Martha, and Lazarus and Simon follow some distance. Presently the Saviour stops, and again says to the sad-hearted women: "Once more, beloved women, fare ye well." Then, turning towards the charmful spot which so often afforded Him repose and shelter from weariness and persecution, He exclaims: "Thou, dear, hospitable Bethany, never again shall I linger in thy quiet valleys." The scene which follows—Jesus taking leave of His mother—is deeply touching. Mary has approached with her friends, whilst her son has been bidding farewell to His friends at Bethany. It may appear strange to the spectator that the mother in the play should be younger than her son; hence it should be borne in mind that, according to the ideas of the Bavarian peasant, the Madonna is possessed of eternal youth. "O dearest Jesus!" exclaims Mary, wringing her hands in agony as she approaches her Son, "full of tender yearning have I hastened with my friends to see Thee once more before Thou goest away." "Beloved mother," tenderly answers the Son, "I am now on the way to Jerusalem. Now, dearest mother, is the time appointed from the beginning to give myself up as a sacrifice according to the Father's will. I am prepared to consummate the work of atonement." "I have forebodings," says Mary; "my heart tells me what kind of a sacrifice that will be." The disciples, who stand around, are deeply affected at this scene. They all are filled with sorrow, except Judas, who is all the while brooding over the waste of ointment, and still mutters to himself, "These three hundred pence would just be enough for me. If I had secured them, I could now live contentedly. No! I will no longer be one of His disciples, but will take the first opportunity of quitting His company." Christ then leaves the scene, followed by His disciples and Lazarus; the women follow the retreating figures with their looks. Simon, bethinking himself of the trust confided to him by the Lord, invites the Virgin and her attendants to enter the house, where they relieve their common sorrow by giving vent to their tears. Thus ends the pathetic, heart-melting scene. The entire act is one of great dramatic interest and importance in the Passion Play. It contains the germs of the betrayal. Envy, selfish, cold, and calculating, takes possession of Judas's soul at the sight of the ointment poured by the penitent woman over the feet of her Lord, and urges him on, spurred by fear for his future material existence, to the deed of betrayal in the Garden of Gethsemane.

ACT IV.—CHRIST'S LAST JOURNEY TO JERUSALEM.

TABLEAU. King Ahasuerus repudiates Vashti and elevates Esther.—Esther i. ii.

QUITTING peaceful Bethany, Christ sets out for Jerusalem, in order that the will of the Father who sent Him be fulfilled. It is His last journey thither. He is going, indeed, to celebrate the Jewish Passover, but He Himself is the Lamb which is to be slain for the sins of the people. This scene is prefigured by the tableau of King Ahasuerus repudiating his haughty queen, Vashti, and elevating Esther in her stead. In like manner Christ is to reject the proud and disdainful Jews, as punishment for their sins, and to elect for Himself a better and more worthy people. Its significance is expressed in the following address of the Choragus:—"*Behold, O people of God, thy Saviour is at hand. The One long promised has come. Hear and follow Him. Blessing and life He will bring. Jerusalem, alas! is blind and deaf. She haughtily rejects the hand offered her; therefore the Most High turns away His face, and leaves her to go down to destruction. Thus in ancient times the disdainful bearing of Queen Vashti, who refused to attend the banquet of her lord and spouse, enraged the king, and caused him to banish her from his presence. He chose a gentler and purer consort to share his throne. Thus, too, will the Synagogue be abolished, and the kingdom of God intrusted to another people—a people that will bring forth fruits of righteousness.*"

Before the tableau is revealed, the Choragus, assisted by the entire Chorus, terminates his preparatory remarks with this solemn warning to Jerusalem:—

Jerusalem! Jerusalem! Erwache! Erkenne was zum Frieden dir noch werden Kann;	Jerusalem! Jerusalem! arise, And hear the voice that speaks to thee of peace;

ACT IV.—CHRIST'S LAST JOURNEY TO JERUSALEM.

Doch zögerst du—so fängt die zeit der Rache,
Unselige! mit fürchterlichen Schlägen an.
Jerusalem! Jerusalem!
Bekehre dich zu deinem Gott!
Verachte nicht mit Frevelspott
   Den Mahnungsruf der Gnade,
Dass nicht, Unselige, über dich
Dereinst in vollen Schalen sich
   Das Höchsten Grimm entlade!
Doch, ach!—ach! die Propheten-Mörderin—
Sie taumelt fort in ihrem bösen Sinn.
Darum, so spricht der Herr,
Diess Volk will ich nicht mehr.

And know, if this last warning thou despise,
Thy day of grace for evermore will cease.
Jerusalem! Jerusalem!
Return unto thy God, return!
Do not, with wicked mockery, spurn
   Of grace the warning cry:
That not in fullest measure be,
Unhappy one, outpour'd on thee
   The wrath of God most high.
Alas! the prophet-murderess
Reels on in her deep wickedness;
The Lord doth say, therefore,
"I'll have this folk no more!"

TABLEAU.—The rising curtain reveals the tableau—King Ahasuerus rejecting Queen Vashti and elevating Esther to the vacated seat. The whole narrative may be read in the book of Esther. King Ahasuerus made a great feast; and Queen Vashti made a feast for the women of his house. On the seventh day, his heart being merry with wine, Ahasuerus commanded his chamberlains to bring Vashti the queen before him, that he might show the people and princes her beauty. But Vashti refused to obey the summons, and the king was very wroth, and by the advice of his wise men, he deprived her of her high position, as a warning to the whole land; and he selected Esther from among the virgins to be his queen. The Chorus sings:—

Seht Vasthi—seht! die Stolze wird verstossen!
Ein Bild, was mit der Synagog der Herr beschlossen.
Entferne dich von meinem Throne,
Du stolzes Weib! unwerth der Krone;
   So spricht Assuerus ganz ergrimmt.
"Dir, schöne Esther! dir sei heute
Zu herrschen an des Königs Seite
   Hier dieser Königsthron bestimmt."
"Die Zeit der Gnade ist verflossen;
Diesz stolze Volk will ich verstossen."
   So wahr ich lebe, spricht der Herr.
"Ein besser Volk wird er sich wählen,
Mit ihm auf ewig sich vermählen,
   Wie mit der Esther Assuer."
Jerusalem! Jerusalem!
Ihr Sünder! höret Gottes Wort!
   Wollt ihr noch Gnade finden,
So schafft aus eu'ren Herzen fort
   Den Sauerteig der Sünden.

Proud Vashti, thou, rejected, dost declare
How the disloyal Synagogue shall fare.
"Depart for ever from the throne,
Learn, Pride! what thou canst call thine own."
   Thus speaks Ahasuerus in his rage:
"Thee, beauteous Esther, we ordain
Next to the king to sit and reign,
   Sharing our royal heritage."
"The time of grace is now gone by,
True as I live," saith God on high!
   "This people proud I will reject,
A better I will choose instead,
With whom eternally to wed,
   As Ahasuerus Esther did elect."
Jerusalem! Jerusalem!
Ye sinners, hear the words divine:
   Would ye still find God's grace?
From out your inmost heart erase
   The leaven of sin malign!

THE JOURNEY TO JERUSALEM.—The opening scene presents Christ and the apostles on their way to Jerusalem. They are passing the brow of Olivet.

Before them lies the Holy City. Christ casts His eyes upon the proud city and weeps over its doom. Peter asks: "Wherefore, Master, art thou so sorrowful?" Jesus answers: "The fate of the unfortunate city goes to my heart." John: "And what will be this fate?" "The days shall come," replies the Saviour, "that her enemies shall cast a trench about her, and compass her, and keep her in on every side, and shall lay her even with the ground, and her children within her walls; and they shall not leave in her one stone upon another" (Luke xix. 43, 44). Andrew, astonished, rejoins: "Why, Lord, will such a fate befall her?" "Because," answers Christ, with a deep, mournful tone, "she knew not the day of her visitation (Luke xix. 44). Alas! this murderess of the prophets, she will also put to death the Messiah. . . . . O Jerusalem, Jerusalem, which killest the prophets, and stonest them that are sent unto thee, how often would I have gathered thy children together, as a hen doth gather her brood under her wings, and ye would not!" (Luke xiii. 34.) The disciples are filled with sorrow at the thought of their Master's proceeding to Jerusalem, as though foreseeing the fate that awaits Him there. He bids Peter and John go to the city to prepare the Passover lamb. To the rest of the disciples He says: "The hour is near in which the Scriptures shall be fulfilled. Accompany me this day for the last time to my Father's house. Let us now follow them to Jerusalem."

THE TEMPTATION OF JUDAS.—During this scene Judas remains at one side of the stage, gloomily brooding over the Saviour's words. He holds in his hand an empty purse; and his thoughts seem still burdened with Mary Magdalene's useless expenditure of the three hundred pence. The future, evidently, appears to him dark, unpropitious. He cannot understand why Christ should leave them; and forebodingly reflects on the results that would necessarily follow if this should come to pass. Finally, no longer able to conceal his selfish fears, he draws near, and addresses the Saviour thus: "But, beloved Master, permit me to suggest—If, indeed, thou dost intend to leave us, do make some provision for our subsistence. See," he adds, holding up the purse, "this will not suffice for over a day longer." "O, Judas," replies Jesus, "trouble not thyself more than is needful." Turning to the others, He adds: "Let us go hence; for I desire to enter once more the house of God." Christ leaves the scene; and, followed by His disciples, except Judas, proceeds to the Holy City. Iscariot remains behind, struggling with the terrible thoughts that have arisen in his mind. In a clear, nervous soliloquy he gives utterance to the train of his ideas, and reveals the germ from which his subsequent betrayal is to develop:—

And shall I follow? I have half a mind.
No roses there will ever bloom for me!
Did not the great deeds of the Master once
Raise hopes of Israel's ancient fame restored?
But this great scheme he seems of late to waive.
His words are all of parting and of death,
He comforts us with dark, mysterious words,
And gives us promise of a future bright
That in the distance gray grows dim and vague.
Long have I fed, too long, upon these dreams,
And hope too long delay'd a loathing brings.
To Him and His, what prospects are held out?
An abject state, and poverty forsooth—

TOBIAS FLUNGER,
THE DELINEATOR OF "CHRIST" IN THE YEAR 1850.

ACT IV.—CHRIST'S LAST JOURNEY TO JERUSALEM.

Ay, and a prison ! I will hie me hence !
It is decided. I'll withdraw : but how ?
Ah ! now I miss that goodly, goodly sum
Of full three hundred pence, profusely spent
For ceremony vain. O, were it mine,—
That were provision for a rainy day !
Now for subsistence I must look about,
And know not where !

Judas has sunk into deep meditation, which is soon followed by still deeper agitation and doubt. He continues to struggle with his own conscience, trying to decide what course to pursue when the spies sent by the Sanhedrim, Dathan, and the other exasperated buyers and sellers of the Temple arrive. Dathan succeeds easily in inducing Judas to accept the terms of the betrayal. The traders then leave, to announce to Caiaphas the unexpected success of their mission. Judas is once more left alone with his conscience, which still gives some signs of life. The prevaricating disciple cannot forget the goodness of the Master towards him. However, avarice gets the upper hand. The unhappy man tries to calm his disquieted conscience by calling to mind the miraculous power of Christ, trusting that He may yet recur to it to save Himself from His enemies. He gives utterance to the tumult and tossing of his soul in the following monologue :—

My word and hand are pledged : and from the deed
I cannot now retreat. Nor were it wise
To cast away this boon which fortune brings,
That without trouble I so well can earn !
My fortune's made. It cannot go amiss.
I'll keep my promise, though I will be paid
Down in advance : then let his priestly foes
Proceed to capture him—and should he fall,
My ship is safely anchor'd with its store.
But if the Master should escape their hands,
As oft before, what then will be my fate ?
What shall I do ? Oh, I will cast me down
Repentant at his feet, for he is good,
And will forgive me for the sin that's pass'd.
Nay, I can safely plead my act was wise—
By which the issue ripen'd. Any how,
I'll take good care to leave a bridge behind,
That, should my forward path obstruction meet,
I can return. The plan is well thought out.
Judas, a clever man thou art ? And yet

I feel ashamed the Master to confront,
For his keen, searching look will pierce my soul,
And will upon my face read every thought.
And all who follow him as I have done
Up to this day will know my heart is false.* * *
It is not so! "Traitor?" That loathsome name
I must not, will not bear!—Traitor ? And yet
I do a harmless thing : the Council asks
At such an hour what the good Master dwells.
And if I tell : 'tis no betrayal false.
Betrayal is—when any one attempts—
No more—Such whims do serve but to perplex.
This maxim, Judas, mark : Whoe'er will gain
An object dear must nerve and muscle strain !

Thus speaking, Judas leaves the stage, taking the road which leads towards Jerusalem. During the preceding transaction we have seen how the germ of avarice gradually developed into a determination to betray the divine Master for a reward in money. Devrient considers this scene one of the best, dramatically considered, of the entire performance. Another scene represents the apostles John and Peter, at the house of Mark, in Jerusalem, whither they were sent to prepare for the coming of Christ to celebrate the Last Supper.

ACT V.—THE LAST SUPPER.

TABLEAU I. The Lord sends manna to the Israelites in the wilderness.—Exodus xvi.
TABLEAU II. The grapes brought by the spies from Canaan.—Numbers xiii. 23.

THE Chorus again takes up its position upon the proscenium, and the Choragus commences as follows:—"*Our Divine Benefactor, about to enter upon the career of His sufferings, urged by the impulse of His infinite charity, provides spiritual nourishment for His children during the time of their pilgrimage on earth. Being Himself prepared to be a sacrifice, He institutes a sacrament that shall proclaim through centuries and to the end of time His love for humanity. With the rain of manna the Lord miraculously fed the children of Israel in the desert, and gladdened their hearts with grapes from Canaan. But Christ offers us a better banquet, one from very Heaven. From His mysterious body and blood grace and bliss flow upon humanity.*" The spectator is thus made acquainted with the significance of the two tableaux prefacing the dramatic scene. After the Choragus has given his lucid explanation, a sweet tenor voice sings the following few lines immediately relating to the dramatic scene:—

Nun nähert sich die Stunde,	The hour foretold of yore draws nigh,
Und die Erfüllung fängt sich an,	And the fulfilment now takes place
Was längst in der Propheten Munde	Of what, by prophets, God most High
Der Herr der Menschheit kund gethan.	Announced in mercy to our race.
An diesem Volke, spricht der Herr,	The Lord doth for this people grieve,
Hab' ich kein Wohlgefallen mehr;	He finds in them no more delight;
Ich will nun keine Opfergaben	Nor can He from their hands receive
Von seinen Händen ferner haben.	Their sacrificial offerings trite.
Ich stifte mir ein neues Mahl:	A covenant new the Lord this day
Diess spricht der Herr :—und überall	Doth make with all who do His will,
Soll auf dem ganzen Erdenrunde	A feast wherein His people may
Ein Opfer sein in diesem Bunde.	A purer sacrifice fulfil.

FIRST TABLEAU.—The tableau representing the rain of manna in the wilderness, which is now revealed, is amongst the finest of the entire Passion Play. More than four hundred persons, including one hundred and fifty children, the youngest of them being not quite three years old, are engaged in forming the various groups of this exquisite picture. The Israelites stand in dense crowds, the children in the foreground; and back of the groups youths and maidens appear. The mothers hold their babes in their arms, whilst aged men fill up the rear. Moses, who is leading the Israelites through the desert, is the most conspicuous figure, and is recognized by means of golden rays upon his head. He holds a staff in his hand which points towards Heaven. After him his brother Aaron, the high-priest, occupies the most prominent position. Every hand is stretched out, and every eye is directed towards Heaven, from which an abundant supply of manna uninterruptedly falls. It comes lightly, like a gentle fall of snow. The

ACT V.—THE LAST SUPPER.

little children in the foreground, standing with their innocent faces turned upwards, and holding out their baskets and aprons to catch the sweet food before it reaches the earth, form a most attractive feature in the scene. While the tableau is revealed, the Chorus sings a charming hymn of thanksgiving. In the second stanza, when the curtain has fallen and the Chorus stand before the audience, they explain the symbolic meaning of the picture as related to the Holy Sacrament:—

Das Wunder in der Wüste Sin	From hands angelic see the manna flow,
Zeigt auf das Mahl des neuen Bundes hin.	And mysteries still deeper faith will show.
Gut ist der Herr, gut ist der Herr :	Proclaim it loud : the Lord is good,
Das Volk, das hungert, sättigt er	He gives His hungering people food :
Mit einer neuen Speise	He, in a wondrous wise,
Auf wunderbare Weise.	Rains manna from the skies.
Der Tod doch raffte alle hin,	Yet they are number'd with the dead,
Die assen in der Wüste Sin	Who 'mid such wondrous signs were fed :
Diess Brod im Ueberflusse ;	Their names have pass'd away.
Des neuen Bundes heilig Brod	Not so who taste the bread of grace ;
Bewahrt die Seele vor dem Tod	They'll shun the ruin of our race
Beim würdigen Genusse.	At the great Judgment Day.

SECOND TABLEAU.—Less effective, perhaps, is the tableau of the grapes from Canaan, in which the same figures appear as in the preceding picture. The messengers sent out as spies by Moses have returned from the land "flowing with milk and honey." Two of their number bear upon a long pole, resting on their shoulders, the ponderous cluster of grapes which they found at Eshcol, and at the sight of which the Children of Israel stand in mute astonishment. While the picture is exhibited, the Chorus explains its principal bearings in song :—

Gut ist der Herr, gut ist der Herr !	Good is the Lord, good is the Lord !
Dem Volke einstens hatte er	Once to His folk He did accord
Den besten Saft der Reben	The best fruit of the vine,
Aus Kanaan gegeben.	From Canaan's land divine !
Doch diess Gewächse der Natur	This luscious sap was sent, indeed,
War zum Bedarf des Leibes nur	To satisfy the mortal need :
Bestimmt nach Gottes Willen.	Such was Jehovah's will.
Des neuen Bundes heil'ger Wein	But the new covenant's sacred wine
Wird selbst das Blut des Sohnes sein,	Will be the Son's own blood divine,
Der Seele Durst zu stillen.	The spirit's thirst to still.
Gut ist der Herr, gut ist der Herr !	Good is the Lord who o'er us lives,
Im neuen Bunde reichet er	Within the covenant new He gives
Sein Fleisch und Blut im Saale	His flesh and blood within
Zu Salem bei dem Mahle.	The hall at Salem's meal !

THE LAST SUPPER.—The celebration of the Passover by Christ and His disciples, and the instituting of the Sacrament of the Lord's Supper, possesses a peculiar interest for all Christians. The lifted curtain reveals a chamber in the house of Mark, into which the Saviour and all the disciples have just entered. They are standing around the table ; while the master of the house and his servant stand at some distance, ready to attend to the wants of their guests. The table is evidently a copy of the one in Leonardo da Vinci's celebrated picture of the Last Supper. The positions taken by the Lord and the twelve, together with many other details, are also in imitation of Da Vinci's same masterly production. After all are seated, Christ finds Himself in the centre, with Peter at His right, and John to His left. To the right of Peter are seated Judas, James the elder, Andrew, Thomas, and Simon; and to the left of John are Bartholomew, Matthew, James the younger, Philip, and Thaddeus. These positions, however, are frequently changed in the subsequent pictures. After the washing of hands, and the lamb and wine have been placed upon the table, Christ begins by prayer: "Father, my heart rises to Thee. These are Thy gifts that I shall now partake of in peace; oh, bless this food with Thy divine blessing!" To His disciples He says, "With desire I have desired to eat this Passover with you before I suffer: for I say unto you, I will not any more eat thereof, until it be fulfilled in the kingdom of God." (Luke xxii. 15, 16.) Christ then raises the cup in the same manner as the food, and again gives thanks, saying: "Father, I thank Thee for this fruit of the vine!" He then passes the chalice to the disciples, adding: "Take this, and divide it among yourselves: for I say unto you, I will not drink of the fruit of the vine, until the kingdom of God shall come." (Luke xxii. 17, 18.) The disciples ask the Master: "Lord, is it then the last time that thou wilt celebrate with us the Passover?" He answers them; "I will drink a new drink with you in the kingdom of God, of My Father. Ye are they which have continued with Me in My temptations. And I appoint unto you a kingdom, as My Father hath appointed unto Me; that ye may eat and drink at My table in My kingdom, and sit on thrones judging the twelve tribes of Israel." (Luke xxii. 28, 30.)

Then arises a dispute among the disciples about the place of honour in the kingdom of the future, which they expect in the earthly sense. Jesus does not answer their questions, but bids the host bring water and a towel, with which to wash the disciples' feet. The apostles, not having understood Christ's words, are astonished, and ask, "What will he do?" Christ places a large white napkin about Him, and then addresses Peter: "Peter, reach hither thy foot." "How? Lord," he exclaims, "dost thou wash my feet?" Christ answers: "What I do, thou knowest not now; but thou shalt know hereafter." Peter saith unto Him: "Thou shalt never wash my feet." Jesus answers him: "If I wash thee not, thou hast no part with Me." Thereupon Peter exclaims: "Lord, not my feet only, but also my hands and my head." Peter willingly removes his sandals, and the ceremony of the washing of the feet is proceeded with. The apostle places a foot in the basin, the servant pours water upon it from an earthen pitcher, and Christ wipes it with the linen-cloth. In like manner the feet of all the disciples are washed, Judas even not being omitted. A peculiar solemnity is lent the occasion by performances of the musicians, who are concealed from view. They sing the following two stanzas of a beautiful composition of Daisenberger's, written during the performances of the summer of 1871, and set to music by the assistant school-teacher of the village :—

JOSEPH MAIER AS "CHRISTUS."

ACT V.—THE LAST SUPPER.

Behold the Lord and Saviour kneel,
O tender love! O mercy sweet!
Despising not, before the meal,
To wash His loved disciples' feet.

O let this deed which He did give
To them be for us, too, a sign;
To practice, while on earth we live,
Such meekness and such love divine.

Having performed this act of humility, Christ returns the linen-cloth to the master of the house, and John assists Him again in putting on His mantle. "Now ye are clean," He then remarks, "yet not all!" These words seem to go home to Judas's heart; for he sits with his head resting in his hand, as if still struggling with his conscience. Then follows the institution of the Holy Sacrament.

Christ first takes the bread, and, lifting it towards Heaven, prays: "O Father, give Thy blessing." He then breaks the food, and gives a portion of it to the disciples in turn, first to Peter, and then to John, placing a piece on the tongue of each, and saying: "Take, eat; this is My body which is given for you: this do in remembrance of Me." Judas, whom the Lord does not pass by, gives visible marks of confusion, and even consternation, when his turn comes. Christ then raises the cup, and, lifting His eyes towards Heaven, gives thanks, and then hands it to them, saying: "Drink ye all of it; for this is My blood of the new testament, which is shed for many for the remission of sins." (Matt. xxvi. 27, 28.) He Himself gives the cup to the disciples in succession, saying: "As often as ye do this, do it in remembrance of Me." After the distribution of the Eucharist Christ resumes His seat. The disciples are deeply moved and afflicted. The qualms of conscience begin to be experienced by Judas; John, the disciple whom Jesus loved, sinks his head upon the Master's breast. Jesus again laments: "Verily I say unto you, one of you which eateth with Me shall betray Me." (Mark xiv. 18.) "Master," simultaneously ask several disciples, "one of the twelve?" "Yea," responds Christ, "it is one of the twelve. He that dippeth his hand with Me in the dish, the same shall betray Me." Even Judas ventures the question: "Is it I?" The remark has not escaped the ear of the Saviour, who replies: "Thou sayest it." John ventures to put the request, but almost in a whisper: "Lord, tell us who it is." And Christ answers him: "He it is to whom I shall give a sop when I have dipped it." Christ dips a sop and gives it to Iscariot, saying: "Judas, that thou doest, do quickly."

Judas, now confused, and conscious that his guilt is discovered by the Master, hastily rises from his seat and rushes out of the room. Christ utters to the remaining eleven the memorable words recorded by the several Evangelists: "Now is the Son of Man glorified, and God is glorified in Him. If God be glorified in Him, God shall also glorify Him in Himself, and shall straightway glorify Him. Little children, yet a little while I am with you. Ye shall seek Me; but whither I go, ye cannot come." Then follows the assurance of Peter, that he will give his life for the Master; but Christ answers: "O Simon! Verily I say unto thee, that this night, before the cock crow, thou shalt deny Me thrice." Christ speaks more of the fate that is suspended over Jerusalem, and concludes with solemn thanksgiving. The whole scene is intensely devotional, solemn, and affecting. When Christ approaches the foreground, we see that He is deeply moved. He remains silent for awhile, His eyes raised towards heaven. The apostles stand around in perfect silence, with faces full of sadness as they gaze upon their sorrowful Master. Christ perceives their distress; and, before leaving the apartment, attempts to comfort them with these words:—

Why are ye all so mournful, dearest children? Why gaze so sadly on your Lord? Let not Your hearts be troubled: ye believe in God, Believe also in Me. My Father's house Hath many mansions, and I go before, There to prepare a dwelling unto you. And I will come again, and you receive Unto Myself, that where I am, ye be. For I would leave you not as orphans here. Peace I leave with you—yea, My peace I give:	Not as the world gives—give I it to you. Keep, O My children, My commands, that ye Love one another, as I you have loved. Hereafter I will not talk much with you. The prince of this world cometh and he hath Nothing in Me. But that the world may know That I do love the Father, and as He Gave Me commandment, even so I do. Arise, My children, let us go from hence.

ACT VI.—THE BETRAYER.

TABLEAU. Joseph sold to the Midianites for twenty pieces of silver.—Gen. xxxvii.

THE Old Testament type of the betrayal of Christ by Judas Iscariot is the selling of their brother Joseph to the Ishmaelite merchants by the sons of Jacob. This is the subject, which presented in the form of a *tableau vivant*, introduces the present act. The Choragus thus explains the relation of the tableau to the act which is to follow:—

"*Alas! false friends have now united with the declared enemies of Jesus. A few pieces of silver suffice to efface all love and fidelity from the heart of Iscariot. Abandoning all, this ungrateful wretch proceeds to make the most shameful bargain; he sells for filthy lucre—the reward of treachery—the best of masters. Similar feelings, alas! once possessed the sons of Jacob, when they mercilessly sold their own brother for an accursed price to the foreign usurers. When the heart pays homage to the idol of lucre, all the nobler feelings are deadened; honour becomes venal, and therewith a man's word, love and friendship.*"

The Chorus continues in song, denouncing selfishness and usury, and would fain restrain Judas from accomplishing his fell deed:—

Wie schaudert's mir durch alle Glieder! Wohin? wohin, O Judas! voller Wuth? Bist du der Schurke, der das Blut Verkaufen wird? Gerechte Rache, säume nicht— Ihr Donner—Blitze stürzet nieder— Zermalmet diesen Bösewicht!	How quake my limbs beneath the spell! O whither, Judas, torn with rage away? Art thou he who the blood will sell? O vengeance just, do not delay! Ye thunders, lightnings, quick descend, And this incarnate demon rend!
Von Euch wird Einer mich verrathen! Und dreimal sprach der Herr diess Wort. Vom Geiz verführt zu schwarzen Thaten, Lief einer von dem Mahle fort; Und dieser Eine—heil'ger Gott!— Ist Judas, der Iskariot.	"One in our midst will Me betray!" Thus spake the Lord to th' chosen few; And avarice led that one astray To deeds commit of darkest hue. And this one man, O sacred God, Was Judas, the Iscariot.

ACT VI.—THE BETRAYER.

Ach Judas ! Judas—welche Sünde !—	Oh, Judas, Judas, have a mind !
Vollende nicht die schwarze That !	O, do not do the deed, we cry !
Doch nein—vom Geize taub und blinde,	But avarice makes him deaf and blind.
Eilt Judas fort zum hohen Rath.	He hurries to the Council High,
Und wiederholt voll bösem Sinn	And there repeats with mind profane,
Was einst geschah zu Dothain.	What once took place on Dothan's plain!

TABLEAU.—The tableau revealed is the continuation of one exhibited in the second act of the Play, and showing the sons of Jacob when they decided to cast their brother Joseph into a well. The fruitful plains of Dothan appear in the distance. In the foreground are assembled the brothers; two of them are concluding the sale of blood with the merchants, the stump of a tree serving as a table on which to transact the business. Young Joseph stands, stripped of his garment of many colours, apparently in the act of defending himself from the brutality of one of his own brethren. The Chorus sings the story of the picture:—

Was bietet für den Knaben ihr?	"Good merchants, tell us if, forsooth,
So sprechen Brüder, wenn euch wir	You are disposed this hearty youth
Ihn käuflich übergeben?	To purchase with your gold?"
Sie geben bald um denn Gewinn	The men consent ; and, at the sight
Von zwanzig Silberlingen hin	Of twenty silver pieces bright,
Des Bruders Blut und Leben.	Young Joseph's life is sold.
Was gebet ihr?—wie lohnt ihr mich?	"What will you give ? What is my pay ?"
Spricht der Iskariot, wenn ich	Iscariot says, "if I betray
Den Meister euch verrathe?	The Lord into your hands ?"
Um dreissig Silberlinge schliesst	For thirty silver pieces he
Den Blutbund er, und Jesus ist	Concludes the bloody work, and see,
Verkauft dem hohen Rathe.	Jesus a captive stands !
Was diese Scene uns vorhält,	And what this scene reveals to you
Ist ein getreues Bild der Welt.	Is of the world a picture true !
Wie oft habt ihr durch eure Thaten	How often by your deeds untold
Auch euren Gott verkauft—verrathen !	Have you your God betray'd and sold ?
Den Brüdern eines Joseph hier,	Ye curse good Joseph's brothers here,
Und einem Judas fluchet ihr,	And over Judas judge austere,
Und wandelt doch auf ihren Wegen ;	Yet walk their ways remiss ;
Denn Reid und Geiz und Bruderhass	For envy, avarice, brothers' hate
Zerstören ohne Unterlass	Destroy man's peace on earth's estate,
Der Menschheit Frieden, Glück und Segen.	And happiness and bliss !

JUDAS BEFORE THE SANHEDRIM.—The plot laid by the Sanhedrim is successfully carried out by the Temple-traders, who, as seen in the preceding act, win Judas by appealing to his avarice. Iscariot, filled with traitorous thoughts, absents himself from the Passover meal, and, as previously agreed, hurries to meet his new friends, in order to secure his reward before commencing the shameful work. Previous to the appearance of the betrayer, however, another meeting of the Sanhedrim, more wild and tumultuous than the former one, is shown. The two high-priests Caiaphas and Annas, preside ; the priests, the pharisees and rabbis, are those who were present before, with the addition of two new members, Nicodemus and Joseph of Arimathea, who are respectively seated at the extreme right and left, and destined to play a significant *rôle* in the future scenes. The members await the arrival of Judas. They strive to excel each other in expressing their desire for revenge, and in ridiculing Jesus, only Nicodemus and Joseph of Arimathea speaking in his favour. Their expressions call out the wrath of Caiaphas, who declares them to be unworthy to remain in the assembly. Now Judas appears, with his empty money-bag, which he hopes to replenish by the betrayal of his Master. While the priests are bargaining with him, one of the high-priests asks him if he will not later regret his action? This question leads the traitor's mind back again to the costly ointment, the three hundred pence, the empty treasury, and the reproaches of the Lord. The members of the Council assure him that he is in the right to take care of himself. They finally agree to give him thirty pieces of silver for the betrayal, and the money is sent for out of the treasury of the Temple. Again does Nicodemus protest; he and Joseph of Arimathea will have no participation in the deed of blood, and leave the room, highly indignant, the other members crying after them that they should join the society of the Galilean. A rabbi then returns with the blood-money. The Council asks Judas to receive his reward. "I am contented," he answers, "and now I can make good my loss." With these words he steps hastily forward to the table, counts, and tries attentively every piece of silver as it is paid out to him, as if distrusting their genuineness. The scene is one of the finest dramatic pictures of the entire play. After all the money has been firmly secured in Judas's money-bag, the Council says to him, "Now thou hast thy reward; now hasten thee!" "To-day," he answers, "he shall be in your hands." He then reveals his plan, desiring the aid of soldiers in order to fall upon Jesus by night, near the brook Kedron. He tells them the sign he will give, *i.e.*, the kiss. All his demands are granted: the dealers of the Temple determine, however, not to lose sight of Judas until the deed is accomplished, and Annas regrets that his old age and weakness prevent him from accompanying the betrayer. The members of the High Council depart with the cry of revenge: "Let him die! let him die! He is the enemy of our fathers!"

ACT VII.—THE GARDEN OF GETHSEMANE.

TABLEAU I. Adam condemned to earn his bread by the sweat of his brow.—Gen. iii. 17.
TABLEAU II. The Rocks of Gibeon; Joab's treachery to Amasa.—2 Samuel xx. 9.

AFTER the Last Supper we are told in the sacred narrative, Christ went with his disciples over the brook Kedron, unto a place called Gethsemane. The present act takes us to the eventful garden, the scene of Christ's mental anguish and tribulation at his approaching sufferings, as well as of the act of betrayal by Iscariot. These two events of the Saviour's life are introduced as usual by Old Testament types: the first, representing Adam condemned to earn his bread by the sweat of his brow, typifying Christ's bloody sweat in the garden on Olivet; the

ACT VII.—THE GARDEN OF GETHSEMANE.

second, Joab giving Amasa a kiss whilst secretly plunging a dagger into his body, an Old Testament parallel to the kiss given by Iscariot to his Master. The Choragus addresses the audience on the relation of type to fulfilment: "*As the getting of bread by the sweat of his brow—a punishment, alas! for his own guilt—bore down Adam's exhausted strength, so do the sins of humanity press heavily upon the heart of the Saviour. Borne down by the immensity of His grief, His head crushed to the ground by the ponderous burden of human sin, His countenance covered with sweat of blood, He fights the terrible fight on Olivet. Already we see the leader of the myrmidons approaching, the traitorous disciple, Iscariot, who shamefully abuses that love which the Saviour has always shown him, by accepting the hangman task of betrayal. Joab, likewise, committed a similar treachery towards Amasa; for, while with hypocritical mien he gave him the kiss of friendship on the cheek, he plunged the dagger's point into his heart.*" The Chorus explains in song the nature of the scene to be enacted as follows :—

Judas, ach ! verschlang den Bissen
  Bei dem Abendmahle
Mit unheiligem Gewissen—
Und der Satan fuhr sogleich in ihn.—
Was du thun willst, sprach der Herr,
Judas !—dieses thu' geschwind.—Und er
Eilte aus dem Speisesaale
In die Synagoge hin
  Und verkaufte seinen Meister.
	Judas, ah, the morsel swallow'd,
	  At the holy sacrament,
	With a conscience all unhallow'd,
	  Satan did his soul ferment.
	"What thou doest," the Lord did say,
	"Judas, do quickly." And away
	He hurried from the evening meal
	To th' synagogue, with miser zeal ;
	And there he sold his Master good—
	  Our Saviour—for the price of blood !

Bald ist vollbracht—bald ist vollbracht,
  Die schrecklichste der Thaten,
Ach ! heute noch, in dieser Nacht
  Wird Judas ihn verrathen,
O kommet Alle,—kommet dann,
Und sehet mit die Leiden an.
	'Twill soon be done, 'twill soon be done,
	  The deed most dire and fell ;
	Before this day its course hath run—
	  Judas his Master sell !
	O come, ye faithful ones, O come,
	And see with us the Sufferer's doom !

Im Schatten erst—und bald im Lichte
  Erscheinet sie—
Die traurigste Geschichte
  Von Gethsemani.
	In shadows first, and then in light,
	  We here shall see
	The story old, as dark as night—
	  Gethsemane.

FIRST TABLEAU.—Gethsemane is typified by the tableau of labouring Adam. The scene is a dreary wilderness, producing thorns and thistles in abundance. Adam, clothed with the skin of a sheep, is engaged in laborious tilling of the ground. Just as the curtain is raised, he is seen resting for a moment, and despairingly pressing his strong hand upon his brow, which is covered with perspiration. Even his children have to bear the fruits of the curse. Three of the older ones are pulling thorny stocks out of the ground ; a task which apparently takes all their strength. To the left is the grieving mother, Eve. She is seated on a rock, and holds her youngest child in her lap ; whilst close beside her, an older one holds a luscious apple in his hand. Another child is hacking the ground ; still another little innocent one is playing with a lamb. The picture is artistic, and exceedingly effective, notwithstanding few anachronistic improprieties of its details. While it is revealed the Chorus sings of its symbolical teachings:—

O wie sauer, O wie heiss,
  Wird es Vater Adam nicht!
Ach! es fällt ein Strom von Schweiss
  Ueber Stirn und Angesicht.
Dieses ist die Frucht der Sünde,
  Gottes Fluch drückt die Natur;
Darum gibt bei saurem Schweisse
Und bei mühevollem Fleisse
  Sie die Früchte sparsam nur.
	See how here the scorching beams
	  Father Adam's woes enhance!
	While hot perspiration streams
	  Down his brow and countenance.
	This is the fruit of sin!
	  Upon the earth God's curse doth rest:
	And though man tries in weary toil
	To wring subsistence from the soil,
	  It sparely yields its fruits at best.

So wird's unserm Jesus heiss,
  Wenn er auf dem Oelberg ringt,
Dass ein Strom von blut'gem Schweiss
  Ihm durch alle Glieder dringt.
Dieses ist der Kampf der Sünde,
  Für uns kämpfet ihn der Herr,
Kämpfet ihn in seinem Blute,
Zittert, bebet; doch mit Muthe
  Trinkt den Kelch der Leiden er.
	And thus were Jesu's woes increased,
	  Which on the Olive Mount he bore;
	A stream of bloody sweat ne'er ceased
	  To flow from ev'ry limb and pore.
	This is the fight of sin!
	  With sin the Lord for us did fight,—
	He fought it with His blood so dear,
	He trembled, quaked, but without fear
	  The cup of sorrow drank outright.

SECOND TABLEAU.—The second tableau represents the story of Joab's treachery towards Amasa, as told in 2 Samuel xx. King David had commanded Amasa to assemble the men of Judah. Amasa, however, tarried longer than the set time allotted him; and David, fearing that Sheba would thereby gain time to "get him fenced cities and escape," ordered Joab to follow him, and get the men of Judah together. "At the great stone which is in Gibeon," he found Amasa, and advanced toward him, to give him the customary greeting, intending the while to slay him, in order to secure the command himself. "Art thou in health, my brother?" he asked Amasa, his rival, who apprehended nothing. "And Joab took Amasa by the beard with the right hand to kiss him. But Amasa took no heed to the sword that was in Joab's hand; so he smote him therewith in the fifth rib, and shed out his bowels to the ground, and struck him not again, and he died." The scene represents the barren rocks of Gibeon, under whose shade the soldiers of the two leaders are resting. Joab and Amasa are apparently embracing, while, in truth, the former, feigning to give his rival the kiss of friendship, is plunging the murderous weapon into his body. The Chorus sings the deep moral lesson of this tableau, its reference to the betrayal by Iscariot, alternating with a second chorus concealed back of the rocks. The effect produced is as if the rocks of Gibeon were made to denounce the treachery committed in their friendly shade:—

Den Auftritt bei den Felsen Gabaon— Den wiederholet Judas—Simons Sohn.	The scene that once took place near Gibeon Doth here repeat Iscariot, Simon's Son.

CHORUS.

Ihr Felsen Gabaon!
Warum steht ihr ohne Zierde—
Sonst des Landes stolze Würde—
  Wie mit einem Trauerflor umhüllet da?
  Saget, ich beschwör' euch, saget: Was
      geschah? Was geschah?
	Ye rocks of Gibeon!
	Why shorn of verdure do ye gloomy stand?
	Ye, once the pride and boast of all the land,
	  As if in mourning ye had veil'd your face?
	  Tell, I beseech you, What took place?
	      What took place?

ACT VII.—THE GARDEN OF GETHSEMANE.

Echo from the Rocks.

Flieht, Wanderer! flieht schnell von hier; Verflucht sei dieser blutgedüngte Ort! Da fiel von einer Meuchlershand durchbohrt Ein Amasa, Bertrauend auf der heil'gen Freundschaft Gruss— Getäuscht durch Joabs falschen Bruderkuss.	Flee, wanderer, flee! Flee quickly from this gloom! Accursed is this blood-stain'd spot of land. Here fell, transpierced by a foul murderer's hand, One Amasa. Too fondly he a greeting friend believed, And Joab's thrust with his embrace received!
O ruft in uns're Stimme :—Der Fluch sei dir! Die Felsen klagen über dich; Die blutgedüngte Erde rächet sich.	O cry with us together: The curse be thine! The towering rocks in wrath complain of thee! The blood-stain'd earth cries out revenged to be!

Chorus.

Verstummet, Felsen Gabaon, mit eurer Stimme, Und hört, und spaltet euch vor Grimme, Ihr Felsen Gabaon! So verräth den Menschensohn. Ach! mit heuchlerischem Grusse Und mit einem falschen Kusse Als der Führer einer Rott' Judas, der Iskariot. Ihr Felsen Gabaon: Vernehmet unsern Schwur, Und fluchet diesem Scheusal der Natur!	Be silent, rocks, your wrathful voice assuage, And list to us, nor rend yourselves with rage. Ye rocks of Gibeon! Like as this treachery here was done, Betray'd is thus God's only Son. The leader of a wicked plot, Judas, the Iscariot, Doth give, with hypocritic mien, To Him the traitor's kiss unclean! Ye rocks of Gibeon! O listen to our solemn oath, And curse this monster all things loath!
Ihm flucht das ganze Erdenrund, Eröffne, Erde, deinen Schlund!— Verschlinge ihn!—der Hölle Feu'r Verzehre dieses Ungeheu'r!	The globe entire pours curses forth On him: O ope thy abysm Earth! Swallow him!—and thou, hell-fire! Consume, eat up, the monster dire!

GETHSEMANE.—A single dramatic scene, exhibited on the proscenium, prefaces the representation of Christ's tribulation in the garden of Gethsemane. Led by the betrayer, the trader Dathan, the four priests and some Roman soldiers, pass hurriedly across the stage, on their mission of treachery. This scene is the prelude to Gethsemane. The curtain being raised, the scene on the Mount of Olives is revealed—a garden extending far in the background of the stage. To the right is a slight elevation; to the left are low rocks and shrubs. Jesus, with His disciples, enters it, conversing, taking Peter, John and James with Him, and bidding the others remain at the entrance. Coming nearer, He says, " My soul is sorrowful unto death: tarry ye here, and watch!" Overcome by anguish at His approaching death, He goes forward a little, and kneeling down, prays, full of earnestness, " Abba, Father, all things are possible unto Thee; take away this cup from Me: nevertheless, not as I will, but as Thou wilt." After this prayer, Christ returns to the three, but finds them all asleep. He admonishes them in a friendly manner, and full of love, to watch and pray with Him. Three times He prays; three times He repeats the admonition to His disciples. After Christ has risen from the third prayer, His countenance is seen with blood coursing over it; and during that scene an angel is seen over Christ's head, giving Him assurance. After ending the third prayer, He returns to the three disciples, and finds them still sleeping; but He simply greets them with the words: "Sleep on now, and take your rest." Peter rouses sufficiently to ask: "What is it, Master?" All three then arise, saying: "See, we are ready!" "Behold!" Christ answers, "the hour is at hand, and the Son of Man is betrayed into the hands of sinners. Arise, let us be going."

The catastrophe is approaching. The clang of arms is heard in the distance, and the disciples whom Christ has left in the background spring terrified to their feet. They hasten towards Christ, as if to seek safety in Him who has so long fed, clothed, and protected them. But He says to them: "Behold, he is at hand that doth betray me." And, while the disciples are anxiously gathering about the Lord, the Roman soldiers, led by Judas, appear in the background of the garden. The priests and pharisees, bearing lanterns and torches, the traffickers and the soldiers, now come into full sight. Judas hastens on before them; and, approaching Jesus, who is standing in the midst of the disciples, exclaims: "O Rabbi, be thou greeted!" and he kisses Him. Christ, in simple earnestness, answers: "Wherefore, O friend, art thou come? Judas, Judas, thou betrayest the Son of Man with a kiss!" Christ advances with wonted majesty toward the soldiers, and asks them in a loud voice: "Whom seek ye?" They shout defiantly, and as one man: "Jesus of Nazareth!" "I am He!" He calmly answers. At these words they are cast to the ground as if by some invisible power. Soldiers and priests are struck with consternation. But Christ, aware that the will of the Father must be fulfilled, says to the hirelings: "Be without fear? Arise! Whom seek ye?"

The Roman captain of the guard, thereupon, commands his men to seize the Saviour; and Malchus, with some of his comrades, advances to execute the order. Christ submits to be bound, but Peter draws his sword and cuts off the ear of Malchus. Christ, however, restrains the disciple; and says to Malchus: "Have no fear about thine ear. Thou art healed." To Peter he says, "Put up again thy sword into its place: for all they that take the sword shall perish with the sword. Shall I not drink the cup which the Father hath given me to drink? Thinkest thou that I cannot now pray to my Father, and He shall presently give me more than twelve legions of angels. But how then shall the Scriptures be fulfilled, that thus it must be." The soldiers surround the Saviour, and the captain bids them: "Bind Him fast, so that He do not escape us." Christ gives Himself up without resistance. The disciples steal away from the scene, one by one, leaving the Master alone. Amid mockery and abuse the Saviour is taken from view.

The soldiers have scarcely disappeared from the scene before the disciples Peter and John emerge from where they have found concealment during their Master's capture. They have witnessed Him bound and led away in chains, and now lament His fate. "Alas," exclaims Peter, "they have now taken Him away—our Friend, our beloved Teacher! I cannot comprehend what has taken place!" Overcome with emotion, he buries his face in the bosom of his youthful companion, and weeps. And with him many among

ACT VIII.—JESUS BEFORE ANNAS.   47

the audience. Here follows this touching dialogue between the two disciples:—

JOHN.
Is this His end?
My Friend, my Teacher, who hath done but good,
Hast Thou this treatment and this fate deserved?
Insult, betrayal!—O the thanks of man!
Ne'er, ne'er on earth was such an one, and now—
He is in fetters!

PETER.
I will follow Him.
O say, John! where, then, have they dragged the Lord
And Master in His fearful chains? O where?

JOHN.
Hast thou not heard? To th' house of Annas—come—
Let us go there together.

A pause of an hour is introduced at this point, in order that players and spectators may partake of refreshment. The drama has already lasted four hours, and full four more must elapse before the close. The majority of the spectators hasten to the homes of the village, to secure their noonday meal; but many there are who require neither food nor drink during this interval, which they consecrate to calm reflection on the great, heart-moving scenes that have been witnessed. They feel themselves elevated into a state of mind in which they prefer to remain to the end. The impression of all that has been witnessed makes many hearts full to overflowing. "The Saviour," says Devrient, "is alone. Peter, who promised to stand by Him till death, could only draw his sword once; and John, who had laid his head so tenderly upon the Master's bosom, saying, 'Where thou art there I shall be,' has fled too. Christ goes alone, filled with immeasurable love, to die for the very men who are abusing Him. His intense, solitary grandeur, first gave me the true idea of the power of dramatic art."

SECOND DIVISION.

FROM THE CAPTIVITY IN GETHSEMANE TO THE RESURRECTION AND ASCENSION.

ACT VIII.—JESUS BEFORE ANNAS.

TABLEAU. Zedekiah smites the prophet Micaiah on the cheek.—1 Kings xxii. 24.

THE firing of the cannon planted in the meadow beneath the Kofel announces that the drama is about to be resumed. At the third detonation the spectators are again in their places. The rays of the sun now come with great force upon the audience. Sweet, melancholy strains announce the approaching Passion. In the morning we followed the Redeemer step by step from His triumphal entry into Jerusalem up to His betrayal and captivity; in the afternoon we follow Him to His crucifixion and death; and, later, to the wondrous scenes of His resurrection and ascension.

The first scene represented in the afternoon is that wherein Christ is brought by the priests and soldiers before Annas. The blow there given him on the cheek by one of the high-priest's servants, because He would not answer, is typified by a tableau representing Zedekiah striking the prophet Micaiah on the cheek because he dared to tell King Ahab the truth. The significant reference of this plastic picture is thus explained by the Choragus: "*O, the fearfulness of this night! Behold the Saviour! See him dragged about from court to court, and everywhere shamefully abused. For a courageous word which the Redeemer answers to Annas, He is rewarded by a wretch who brutally strikes Him in the face, in the hope of thus gaining himself praise. Micaiah, too, received the same ignominious treatment for revealing the truth to King Ahab. Truth, alas! is but too frequently rewarded with hatred and persecution. Still, however much its light may be shunned or banished, it will prove victorious at last, and illuminate the darkness.*" The entire Chorus sings of the approaching sufferings of the Saviour:—

Begonnen ist der Kampf der Schmerzen—	Begun, the fight of anguish sore,
Begonnen ist Gethsemani.	Begun is now Gethsemane;
O Sünder! nehmet es zu Herzen	O sinner, ponder calmly o'er
Vergesset diese Scene nie!	The lessons of this agony.
Für euer Heil ist das geschehen,	These scenes of pain on Olive's Mount
Was auf dem Oelberg wir gesehen.	Were borne by Christ on your account.
Für euch betrübt bis in den Tod	For you, the blood-like sweat did steep
Sank er zur Erde nieder,	His every limb at every breath;
Für euch drang ihm, wie Blut so roth,	For you, press'd down in sorrow deep,
Der Schweisz durch alle Glieder.	He suffer'd till He sank in death.
Begonnen ist der Kampf, &c.	Begun, the fight of anguish sore, &c.

TABLEAU.—The tableau is revealed, showing a hall with two thrones: on the one sits Ahab, king of Israel; on the other Jehoshaphat, king of Judah. King Ahab had allied himself (1 Kings xxii.) with Jehoshaphat against the king of Syria, and had determined to inquire of his prophets as to the probable success of such an expedition. "Shall I go against Ramoth-gilead to battle?" he asked of the prophets of Baal, "or shall I forbear?" And they said, "Go up; for the Lord shall deliver it into the hands of the king." But Jehoshaphat inquired for a prophet of the Lord, and Micaiah was sent for. But this prophet told the king of Israel that the Lord had put a lying spirit in the mouth of all these prophets, and that the Lord had spoken evil concerning him, and prophesied the monarch's death. It was for this that the enraged Zedekiah smote him on the cheek. The prophet of Baal is represented as a small, deformed and repugnant figure, as a striking contrast to the venerable Micaiah, according to the characteristic of the Ammergauers in contrasting good and evil. While the picture is revealed the Chorus sings:—

ACT VIII.—JESUS BEFORE ANNAS.

Wer frei die Wahrheit spricht,	Who dares the truth to speak
Den schlägt man in's Gesicht.	Must bear the smitten cheek!
Michäas, er wagte es die Wahrheit laut zu sagen	Micaiah dared to speak the truth out bold; For this was smitten on the cheek, behold!
Und ward in's Angesicht geschlagen.	
König, du wirst unterliegen,	"O King, should Ramoth lead the fight,
Solltest Ramoth du bekriegen,	Thine hosts in battle he will smite."
Diess ist, was Michäas spricht.	Thus said Micaiah wise:
Dich von Unglück dann zu retten,	"Heed not what Baal's prophets teach,
Glaube, König, Baals Propheten—	With wily tongue and subtle speech,
Dieser Schmeichler Lügen nicht!	Heed not their flattering lies."
Doch die Wahrheit des Michäas	But the truth of good Micaiah
Schmeichelt einem Achab nicht;	Did not find with Ahab grace,
Und der Lügner Sedekias	And the liar Zedekiah
Schlägt dafür ihn in's Gesicht.	Smote him rudely on the face.
Lügner, Heuchler, Schmeichler pflücken	Flatterers, liars, hypocrites,
Rosen, Lorbeer ohne Müh'!	Eas'ly pluck them laurels high;
Nur die Wahrheit muss sich bücken,	Only truth to stoop submits;
Denn die Wahrheit schmeichelt nie.	For the truth can never lie!
Jesum über seine Lehren,	Who unto Annas doth the right permit
Seine Thaten zu verhören,	In judgment o'er the Lord supreme to sit?
Räumt das Recht sich Annas ein.	"To know what I have said;" the Lord doth say,
Um zu wissen, was ich lehrte,	"Ask those who heard my teachings day by day."
Frage Jeden, der mich hörte,	
Wird die Rede Jesu sein.	
Doch die Wahrheit auf die Fragen	But the truth, so it is written,
Schmeichelt einem Annas nicht;	Made with Annas no advance;
Und die Unschuld wird geschlagen—	Innocence was here too smitten—
Jesus in das Angesicht.	Jesus on the countenance.

CHRIST BEFORE ANNAS.—After the Chorus has disappeared, we see the high-priest Annas on the balcony of his house. He is impatiently awaiting the Roman soldiers with the captive Nazarene. He is greatly pleased at their success so far, and blesses the hour in which he first heard of Christ's capture. He cries out to Judas, who has passed by with a number of others, "Thy name shall stand in our annals for all time." But Judas begins to evince a palpable dislike to the business he has got into; he begins to tremble at what he has done, fears for the future, and will not bear upon himself any responsibility, saying, "I will not be answerable for his blood." The others answer, ironically, "He is now in our power." In the meantime we hear loud mockery and laughter. The Roman soldiers appear with the bound Saviour, and press Him forward with great brutality. The procession stops before the house of Annas, and Jesus is led upon the balcony, while the infuriated multitude remains below. The hearing commences; but Christ refuses to answer all the questions put to Him by Annas. When asked why He will not speak, He answers, with great dignity: "I spake openly to the world; I ever taught in the Synagogue, and in the Temple, whither the Jews always resort; and in secret have I said nothing. Ask them which heard me what I have said unto them: behold, they know what I said." (John xviii. 20, 21.) It is then that Bulbus strikes the captive in the face, saying: "Answerest thou the high-priest so?" (v. 22.) With calm majesty Christ turns towards the rude offender, yet without looking at him, and says: "If I have spoken evil, bear witness of the evil: but if well, why smitest thou me?" (v. 23.) The calm dignity and self-possession maintained by Jesus enrages Annas, who excitedly asks his captive: "Still wilt thou bid us defiance, even when thy life or death rests in our hands? Lead him away! Take him to Caiaphas, for he is the high-priest. I am tired of this miscreant." He motions that the captive be led out of sight, and continues: "I will go and rest awhile, or rather consider how to bring this beginning to a successful end. But do not forget to call me to the Council at early morning." The high-priest retires, and the soldiers lead Christ away to the palace of Caiaphas, cursing their victim, and pushing Him rudely along before them. The two disciples, Peter and John, approach the proscenium. They are conversing in a low tone, and anxious to learn the fate of the Lord.

ACT IX.—CHRIST BEFORE CAIAPHAS.

TABLEAU I. Naboth sentenced to death on false accusations.—1 Kings xxi. 13.
TABLEAU II. Job in affliction, derided by his wife and friends.—Job ii. 9.

IN the preceding act, Annas commanded the captive to be taken before Caiaphas. The incident is introduced by two Old Testament types, both of which have a prophetic reference to scenes that occurred at the ecclesiastical trial. Naboth is stoned to death, after being sentenced on the testimony of false witnesses; and Job, in his humiliation, is scoffed and reviled by his own friends. The Choragus thus explains their typical significance: "*Before His enraged foes, who are now His judges, the Lord remains silent, and bears with forbearance and patience the accusations and lies brought against Him, and even the sentence of death passed upon Him. Naboth, unrighteously persecuted, was sentenced to death as a blasphemer on the testimony of false witnesses. So, too, is Jesus unjustly condemned,—He whose only guilt is truth, love, and good works. Soon ye will see Him surrounded by base, inhuman hirelings, given over to ridicule and brutality, jeered, maltreated by His enemies. In the picture of patient Job, who suffered the greatest tribulation, and was mocked and insulted by his own friends, we see prefigured the heavenly mildness and forbearance of the beloved Saviour.*" Then, reviewing the past, the Choragus sings :—

Wie blutet mir das Herz!	My heart is bleeding; for, behold! in bands
Der Heiligste steht vor Gericht.	The Lord before His ruthless judges stands!
Musz er der Sünder Bosheit tragen;	Foully betray'd, insulted by His foes,
Verrathen und beschimpft—gebunden und geschlagen:	He bears in silence more than human woes.
Wem zittert nicht im Auge eine Thräne?—	To Annas first, and then to Caiaphas led,
Von Annas weg zu Kaiphas fortgerissen—	While Jews loud clamour that His blood be shed,
Was wird er da, ach! leiden müssen!	A scene to draw from every heart a sigh,
Seht hier im Bilde diese neue Leidensscene.	And force the tears to flow from every eye.

JOHANN LANG (CAIAPHAS).

JOHANN DIEMER (CHORAGUS).

GREGOR LECHNER (JUDAS).

JOSEPH MAIER (CHRIST).

PLAYERS OF 1880.

ACT IX.—CHRIST BEFORE CAIAPHAS.

FIRST TABLEAU.—The Chorus separates and retires, to direct the gaze of the audience upon the tableau of Naboth stoned to death. King Ahab had desired to possess the condemned man's vineyard, because it was a desirable property, and adjoined the royal palace. But Naboth refused to part with the inheritance of his fathers. Ahab was vexed at the refusal, and would not be comforted. While in this state of mind, his queen, Jezebel, approached him, and said: "Dost thou not govern the kingdom of Israel? Arise, and eat bread, and let thine heart be merry: I will give thee the vineyard of Naboth the Jezreelite." In order to get possession of the land for her husband, Queen Jezebel wrote in the king's name "to the elders and nobles of the city, dwelling with Naboth, saying: Proclaim a fast, and set Naboth on high among the people: and set two men, sons of Belial, before him, to bear witness against him, saying: Thou didst blaspheme God and the king. And then carry him out, and stone him, that he may die." The elders and nobles did as the queen commanded, and when the good man was dead, Ahab obtained possession of the coveted vineyard. The tableau is artistically arranged. In it Naboth is being stoned to death, and the dramatist makes Queen Jezebel witness the scene. While the picture is exhibited the Chorus sings:—

Es sterbe Naboth! fort mit ihm zum Tod! Gelästert, König! dich, gelästert hat er Gott:	"Let Naboth die! He blasphemes God on high! Blasphemes the King! He hath deserved to die!
Er sei vertilgt aus Israel! So geifern wild die Lästerzungen— Von einer losen Jezabel Zu einem falschen Eid gedungen.	Let's rid him out of Israel! Thus the blasphemers foam and swear— Hired by the wicked Jezebel 'Gainst Naboth witness false to bear.
Ach! mit dem Tode rächet man, Was Naboth nie verbrochen;— Der Weinberg wird dem König dann Von Schurken zugesprochen.	Lo, Naboth must, thus stoned, expire, For sins that he hath never done; The vineyard, by the wretches dire, Is then the king bestowed upon.
Diesz ist ein treues Bild der Welt, So geht's noch öfters heute. Das arme fomme Lämmchen fällt Dem starken Wolf zur Beute.	This of the world's a picture true, Thus do we find it oft to-day; The gentle lamb falls oft unto The stronger wolf an easy prey!
Ihr mächt'gen Götter dieser Welt— Zum Wohl der Menschheit aufgestellt— Vergeszt bei Uebung eurer Pflicht Des unsichtbaren Richters nicht!	Ye gods so mighty on this earth, Placed over man by rank or birth, Amid your duties ne'er forget The Judge unseen above you set.
Bei ihm sind alle Menschen gleich, Sie mögen dürftig oder reich, Geadelt oder Bettler sein;— Gerechtigkeit gilt ihm allein.	With God all men a hearing find, If rich or poor, if lord or hind; If noble or if beggar grim,— Justice alone belongs to Him.

SECOND TABLEAU.—The second tableau embodies the story of Job's affliction. The central figure of the picture is the afflicted patriarch, covered with wounds and sores. His three friends, who come to mourn with him in his sorrow, and to comfort him, weep at his fate while yet afar off, and his wife, supported by her servants, reproaches him with scorn, and bids him

"Curse God and die!" The Chorus refer continually in the subsequent song to the prophetical significance of the tableau, applying the refrain of "Ach, welch ein Mensch!—Behold the Man!"—first to the typical and then to the Divine Sufferer:

Seht! welch ein Mensch! Ach! ein Gerippe Ein Graus—ein Ekel der Natur. Wie windet sich um Wang und Lippe Ein ausgedörrtes Häutchen nur.	Behold the man! A skeleton! A fright, an object shunned by all. The wither'd skin that hangs upon His cheeks and lips, doth us appal!
Seht! welch ein Mensch! Ach! wie geschunden Sieht man bis auf das Mark hinein. Das Eiter träuft aus seinen Wunden. Und Fäulung frisst schon sein Gebein:	See, what a man! With wounds all o'er! We shudder as we hear his moans; Foul matter runs from every sore And rottenness eats up his bones!
Ach! welch ein Mensch! Ein Job in Schmerzen Ach! wem entlockt er Thränen nicht! Sein Weib doch—seine Freunde scherzen Und spotten seiner in's Gesicht.	Behold the man! A Job in pain! Ah, who can here restrain his tears; His wife and e'en the servile train, Deride his grief, with scoffs and jeers!
Ach! welch ein Mensch! Wer mag ihn einen Menschen nennen? Vom Fusse hin bis an sein Haupt Wird aller Zierde er beraubt.	Behold the man! Who can in him The human form divine still trace? Where find we in his face or limb The wreck of manhood's earlier grace?
Ach! welch ein Mensch! Ihr Augen! weinet heisse Thränen. Ach! Jesus—ach! ein Mensch nicht mehr! Der Menschen Spott und Hohn wird er.	Behold the Man! O let your grief Find in your streaming tears relief. Ah, Jesus, ah, a man no more— The scoffs and jeers of men He bore!
Ach! welch ein Mensch! O alle ihr gerührten Herzen! Ach! Jesus, Jesus! Gottes Sohn Wird loser Knechte Spott und Hohn Bei endelosem Kampf der Schmerzen. Ach! welch ein Mensch!	Behold the Man! See kindly hearts, God's only Son Is scoff'd and scorn'd by every one! To death condemn'd by men profane, He fights the bitter fight of pain. Behold the Man!

JESUS BEFORE CAIAPHAS.—The soldiers, taking their Captive to the house of Caiaphas, are heard in the distance. They are laughing, shouting, and ridiculing his teachings. They disappear through the doorway leading into the palace of Pilate. In a moment the central curtain is raised, and an apartment in the house of the high-priest is exposed to view. In the background of the room is a kind of throne, before which Caiaphas himself stands, surrounded by priests and Pharisees. The zealotic high-priest no longer wears the robes of his office. He is as excited as when haranguing the Sanhedrim. He thanks the four members of the Council for their zeal in aiding to capture the Nazarene. He says there is to be an extraordinary assembly of the Sanhedrim; that matters must be pushed forward with as much dispatch as possible; that the high-priest is busy preparing the necessary witnesses; and that, the sentence of death over the Galilean once spoken, everything is prepared for its execution to be quickly carried out. Caiaphas then commands the priest Samuel to bring in the witnesses, and the soldiers to lead the prisoner before him. Christ, bound as before described, is led in

ACT IX.—CHRIST BEFORE CAIAPHAS.

by Selpha and two soldiers. The priest Samuel and his ready-instructed witnesses, five in number, enter from the opposite side, and the trial commences. "Lead him nearer," Caiaphas says to the soldiers, "that I may look him in the face." After listening to the witnesses, Caiaphas addresses Christ: "Thou hast, therefore, boasted of possessing supernatural, godlike power. Refute them if thou canst! . . . I see very well that thou thinkest, by remaining silent, to free thyself of the charges. Thou darest not acknowledge before thy judge what thou hast taught the people. If thou darest, so hear—I, the high-priest, conjure thee by the living God—tell us: art thou the Messiah, the Son of the living God?" Still He holds His peace.

"Divinely beautiful," says Miss Patruban, "He stands before his judge, although in bonds. The noble head is erect, but the eyes are cast to the ground, as He answers: 'Thou hast said: nevertheless I say unto you, Hereafter shall ye see the Son of man sitting on the right hand of power, and coming in the clouds of heaven,'" (Matt. xxvi. 64.) These words exasperate Caiaphas. He considers them blasphemous; and, in his passion, he tears open the breast of his garment, saying: "What further need have we of witnesses? Behold, now ye have heard his blasphemy. What think ye?" The assembled priests answer as with one voice: "He is guilty of death." (vs. 65, 66.) "Unanimously," Caiaphas exclaims, "is the man pronounced guilty of death. Not I, not the High Council, but the divine law pronounces upon him the judgment of death. I ask you, chief teachers of the law," addressing the priests at his left, "what doth the law say of one who doth not obey the authorities placed over him by God?" The law is read. "Take him," exclaims Caiaphas. "Guard him!" he says to the soldiers, "and at dawn bring him again to the Sanhedrim." He motions imperiously that the captive be taken away. After the soldiers, the witnesses, and the Saviour have disappeared he congratulates the priests on their success. "It is arranged," he says, "that a grand council be held early in the morning; and as soon as the sentence is confirmed by the Sanhedrim, we will hasten to Pilate, that he cause the sentence to be carried out at once."

The curtain falls; but is soon raised again, to reveal the anteroom of the Sanhedrim, where the soldiers abuse their captive while waiting the arrival of the members of the High Council. This short interval is made use of by the Ammergau dramatist to introduce Judas once more. The traitor already feels the sting of conscience. He passes rapidly across the stage, muttering these words, which give us an index to the dark despair that is beginning to fill his soul:—

Forebodings fearful give me never rest.
Those words of Annas: "He must die!
   Must die
E'en 'fore the feast!" ring loudly in mine
   ear.
They will not dare to carry things so far!
Nay, 'twould be fearful if they should!
   And thou,
Unhappy Judas,—thou the traitor vile!

Away grim thoughts! So far it will not
   come!
They will not dare condemn the Innocent!
But I will learn i'th house of Caiaphas how
Matters are standing with the Master's fate;
I can no longer bear these fears and hopes,
I must find out the certainty at once—
I must—for there is no escape, and oh!—
It cannot be that I should hear the worst.

PETER DENIES CHRIST.—It is early morning. The soldiers who have charge of Jesus are waiting for the high-priest in a spacious hall of Caiaphas' palace. The maids are about to light the fire; they scoff at the Saviour even more than the soldiers themselves. Peter and John approach; John enters among the soldiers, but Peter, fearful, remains outside, until John has proved that the way is clear. Finally Peter enters, and begins to warm himself by the fire. One of the maids recognizes Him as a disciple of Christ. The hour of trial proves Peter's weakness; he denies all knowledge of Jesus; and the cock crows for the first time. For the third time he denies the Master, saying, "I do not know this man of whom ye speak!" The cock crows a second time. Peter now recalls the words of the Master whilst at the Last Supper: "Before the cock crow twice thou shalt deny me thrice." Overcome with the consciousness of his guilt, and despairing at his own weakness, he would gladly hasten from the scene. But Malchi, who has entered the hall from the interior of the palace, to call the soldiers to arms and to make ready for the reception of the captive, recognizes Peter at once. "What!" he exclaims. "Have I not seen thee in the garden close beside him, when the ear of Malchus was cut off from his head." There is a sudden commotion among the soldiers, who stand erect, and to their arms, as the Captive is brought into the hall. "He is sentenced to death," says Selpha, in answer to the questions of the soldiers, who exclaim: "O, poor king!" The Saviour's eyes first fall upon Peter. He gazes full of sorrow and sympathy at the conscience-stricken disciple, who stretches out his hand towards Him as if to ward off that penetrating gaze; he covers his face with his hands, and leaves, "weeping bitterly."

The curtain is raised to reveal Christ guarded by the soldiers. The Captive, bound and helpless, is at the mercy of His gaolers—the object of their rude wit and treatment. Clarus says: "Great as is the brutality with which Christ is treated, His calm carriage, firm nobility, and the elevated dignity in His conduct never waver. Even the brutal blows of the soldiers, who wish to make Him stumble, are borne with unconquerable firmness and patience. No unskilfulness and no exaggeration disharmonizes His part, even when, with His hands tied behind His back, the hirelings push Him off His seat upon the floor. During the whole scene the thought is ever present that in spite of all disgrace heaped upon Him, it is here the King of Heaven that suffers; in all these hours of outrage, Christ appears as a lofty victor, and His person wins thereby in dignity and glory." The soldiers, while abusing their Captive, make use of a doggerel rhyme very similar to that found in the versions of the play belonging to the seventeenth century:—

MALCHI.
[*Striking Christ in the face.*]
Come, be so good and say to me,
Who is the rogue that striketh thee?

ABDAS.
If thou art wise enough to know,
So say (*strikes Him*) if I did give the blow?

MALCHI.
[*Shakes Him rudely, and pushes him from the stool.*]
Hear'st thou? Art gone to sleep? Just wait!
I'll punish thee, thou lazy pate!

JACOB HETT AS "ST. PETER."

ACT IX.—CHRIST BEFORE CAIAPHAS.

BERI.
O, great misfortune we bemoan,
The king hath fallen from his throne!

ABDAS.
O woe, O woe! I much regret,—
No more such king as this we'll get!

MALCHI.
[*To Christ, while He is still on the ground.*]
Thou hast such wondrous pranks once play'd;
Canst help thyself without our aid?

PANTHER.
Say, what shall we do next, good men?

ALL.
O, set him on his throne again.

PANTHER.
[*Placing Christ rudely on the stool.*]
Come, glorious monarch, thou shalt see
What reverence deep we'll show to thee.

DAN.
[*Who has been sent by Caiaphas.*]
How go'th it with the new king's fame?

ALL.
He is no good: is sad and tame.

The soldiers are interrupted in their work of abuse by the arrival of Caiaphas' messenger, who brings word that the High Council is assembled, and awaiting the prisoner. The curtain falls as Christ is being led to one of the inner apartments of the palace, where His trial is to take place.

A dramatic portraiture closes this act. Peter, filled with mortification at having denied his Lord and Master, appears once more, to express his contrition for the error he has been led to commit in a season of weakness. When he has poured out his repentance, he leaves the scene; when John, too, appears once more, in search of his fellow-disciple. The monologues spoken by both disciples are from the blank verse edition of the Passion Play written by Pastor Daisenberger:—

PETER.
Alas, my Master! I have deeply fallen!
O woe is me, a mortal weak, infirm!
I have denied Thee, thrice denied Thee, Lord!
O 'tis not possible; for thou know'st well
I was determined to go on with Thee
E'en unto death, and now—O deep disgrace,—
Trusting a reed when I did make the vow—
I have renounced Thee, in ignoble fear.
A base apostate, fugitive I stand
Before my God, before myself abased,
Nor worthy Thy disciple to be called.
My Lord, my Master, hast thou still for me
Mercy in store, and that reviving grace
For sinful man provided in Thy love,—
O let their balsam in my heart be pour'd,
May Thy hand raise me from this deep abyss.
O, execrably weak and changeful mind,
This day, this deed, for ever will I rue,
With penance, till I sink into the grave.
Beloved Master, hear, O hear once more
The pleading voice of my repentant heart;
For nevermore will I forsake Thee, Lord.
God all-forgiving, Thou hast ever shown
Mercy to those who come with contrite heart,
O grant me pardon for my weak denial.
Nay, I have read forgiveness in Thy looks;
That long, sad gaze of sympathy with which
Thou look'dst at me, thine erring, fallen child,
Gave me sweet promise of Thy pardon soon.
Forgive, forgive me, Lord, and from this hour
My whole heart's love shall e'er belong to Thee.
And I will cling to Thee, and from henceforth
Nor earth nor hellish malice shall prevail
To tear me from Thee—Lord, O Lord, forgive!   [*Leaves the proscenium.*]

JOHN.
[*Entering from the left side.*]
But Peter, where is he? Mine eye doth search

For him in vain the busy crowd among !
God grant no trouble hath befallen him.
Hence on the road to Bethany, fair home,
There I, perchance, may meet him on the
    way.

But thou, oh sweetest mother of the Lord !
How sore will thine affliction be, how deep !
When of the latest hours the deeds I tell.
O Judas, Judas, what, what hast thou done?
    [*He follows Peter.*

ACT X.—THE DESPAIR OF JUDAS.

TABLEAU. Cain tortured by his conscience ; a wanderer on the earth.—Gen. iv. 10-17.

THE scene depicting the despair of Judas, on discovering too late that he has given the Master over to death, is prefigured in the tableau of Cain's remorse after the death of Abel. Cain, the fratricide, is represented as in wild anxiety, hurrying hither and thither upon the face of the earth, bearing with him everywhere the murderer's brand on his brow. The Choragus addresses the audience, as usual, on what is to come. " *Why,*" he asks, " *doth Judas wander about so abject and confused? The bitings of a wicked conscience martyr him! The guilt of blood weighs upon the soul that wanders in the fire of the reward of sin.*" Then, as if to warn Judas, and induce him to repent of what he has done, he continues: " *Weep, O Judas, at the crime thou hast committed. O, erase it with tears of penitence. Meekly hoping, plead for grace, for the door of salvation is sti'l open to thee. Oh, woe! The most bitter regret tortures him! Not a single ray of hope penetrates the darkness, and he cries out in anguish with Cain the fratricide:* ' *Too great, too great is my sin!*' *Uncomforted and unpenitent, terror and despair have seized him—the final reward of sin, which drives all its victims towards such a fate.*" The Chorus continues in song :—

O weh dem Menschen ! sprach der Herr
  Der mich wird übergeben ;
Es wäre besser ihm, wenn er
  Erhalten nie das Leben.

Und dieses Weh, das Jesus sprach,
  Folgt Judas auf dem Fusse nach.

In vollen Schaalen wird es sich ergiessen.
  Laut schreit um Rache das verkaufte
    Blut,
Gegeisselt von dem nagenden Gewissen,
Gepeitscht von allen Furien der Wuth,

Rennt Judas rasend schon umher
  Und findet keine Ruhe mehr.
Bis er, ach ! von Verzweiflung fortgerissen
  Hinwirft von sich in wilder Hast
Des Lebens unerträglich schwere Last.

" Woe to that man," thus spake the Lord,
  " Who shall the Son of Man betray ;
'Twere better had his form abhorr'd
  Ne'er come into the light of day."

In fullest measure doth the traitor feel,
  The blighting woe Christ utter'd at the
    meal.
He flees the torment that is ever nigh :
Loud for revenge the blood betray'd doth
    cry ;
Harass'd by doubts and by his conscience
    stung,
He feels the lash by all the furies swung.

Accurs'd Iscariot, torn by deep despair,
  Earth hath no blessings : shame alone his
    share !
At last, soul-broken in the unequal strife,
He breaks the band that holdeth him to life.

TABLEAU.—The tableau is revealed. Two sacrificial altars have been erected by the brothers ; with Abel's offering the descending flame proves that

ACT X.—THE DESPAIR OF JUDAS.

it is well-pleasing to God, whilst the other stands desolate, and excites Cain to slay his more favoured brother. Slain Abel lies stretched upon the ground, close to the altar. Before him, as if about to flee from the sight and his own conscience, stands the murderer. Cain's right hand is pressed on his feverish brow, as if in mad despair, while from the enfeebled grasp of his left hand the murderous club falls to the ground. Pointing to the scene, the Chorus sing the terrible lesson of the tableau:—

So flieht auch Kain. Ach, wohin!	Thus, too, fleeth Cain. But whither? See!
Du kannst dir selbst doch nicht entflieh'n.	Thou canst not from thy conscience flee—
In dir trägst du die Höllenqual;	May'st hasten on from place to place,
Und eilest du von Ort zu Ort,	The scourge ne'er tireth in the race:
Sie schwingt die Geissel fort und fort.	In thee thou bear'st the pains of hell;
Wo du bist, ist sie überall;	Where thou—there is the scourge as well.
Und nie entrinnst du deiner Pein.	This shall the sinner's mirror be:
Diess soll der Sünder Spiegel sein;	From punishment thou canst not flee:
Denn kommt die Rache heute nicht—	If vengeance do not come to-day,
Wird noch der Himmel borgen;	The heavens still can borrow;
So fällt das doppelte Gericht	The double judgment will but stay
Auf ihre Häupter morgen.	To crush thee on the morrow!

JUDAS'S DESPAIR.—Cast off by those who seduced him to crime, Judas appears alone, persecuted by the qualms of his conscience. Terrible are the workings of anxiety, rue, and despair upon the nervous frame of the betrayer. It is as if his whole being were rent by internal discords. Masterly and dramatic is the scene—this beginning of despair:—

Alas, at last, then, have my dreadful fears
And grim forebodings grown to dismal truth?
Yea, troth, Caiaphas sentenced Him to death,
And the High Council this dark deed approves.
Too late! salvation's hope from me hath fled!
What thought, O wretched man, can I now seize?
I who did give him to their blood-stain'd hands!
The price of treason—
         [*Glancing at the money.*
         I will give it back—
And they my Master must return to me!
This very moment to the court I'll go,
And Him demand—but woe, O woe is me!

Could I still save Him? But how vain the hope!
They will but mock me for my tardy rue.
I see beforehand they will but me jeer.
Accursed Synagogue! Thou, thou alone
My heart hast tempted, through thy trading gang,
Who well conceal'd their bloody plans and thine,
Until the Victim in thy net was safe.
With words chastising I will me torment:
Ye, unjust judges, nought, nought will I know
Of your decisions base, Satanical!
Clean shall my hands be of the blood of Him,
Of Him, the Guiltless! O, the torturing qualms,
The pains of hell that burn my inmost soul.

The curtain of the central stage is raised, and reveals the meeting of the Sanhedrim, which has been specially called for early morning. All the members are there, with the exception of Joseph of Arimathea and Nicodemus. Caiaphas and Annas occupy their accustomed, elevated seats.

Judas rushes into the assembly, seeking refuge from the sense of guilt burdening his conscience. The betrayer is told, coolly, to be quiet But he answers, enraged, "No quiet for me! Ye have made me a betrayer. Release again the innocent one. My hands shall be clean!" But the high-priests are deaf to all that Judas says. Judas here develops his greatest dramatic power. Enraged and penitent, he casts the money-bag at the feet of the high-priests, cursing his partners in the crime, "So shall ye, too, fall with me into the abyss!" He rushes headlong out of the hall. The High Council commands that the money be picked up; but since it is blood-money they conclude not to put it again into the treasury, but to buy with it a burial-place for strangers—the "field of blood." They then conclude to do all in their power to hasten Christ's death, before the approaching festival. Jesus says: "From this time on will the Son of man sit in his glory at the right hand of the Father." But they cry, confident of their victory: "The whole world shall speak of us, and of our victory over the Galilean." In order to hasten the execution of the sentence they have pronounced, three members of the Council go to Pilate. But Pilate is a heathen, and his palace is at the same time the judgment-hall. In order not to make themselves unclean, they do not enter Pilate's house, but request a meeting with the Roman governor in the garden. The doorkeeper at Pilate's house makes a quaint remark: "O ye cunning knaves, who swallow camels and strain at gnats!"

The curtain of the central stage is again raised. The scene represented is the field of blood—the place of burial for strangers—a wild spot near to Jerusalem. In the centre is a small mound, overshadowed by a tree with leafy top. Judas appears; passes on hastily; seems greatly confused and excited, as if battling with the stingings of his conscience, finding nowhere rest for body or soul. In his despair, he cries out: "I can no longer endure the torture of my conscience. He warned me before, the good Master! My treachery hath for ever excluded me from the company of His disciples. For me there is no hope, no forgiveness, no salvation!" Yet he finds some comfort in calling to mind the mildness and love which Jesus always manifested towards him, even after he had been meditating the deed of betrayal. He resolves to throw himself at the Master's feet, and beg for forgiveness. But demon-like feelings suddenly get the mastery of him, and he again exclaims: "My sin is too great, that I could expect to receive His forgiveness. No, for me there is neither forgiveness nor salvation!" In this state of excitement and despair, he beats his breast and wrings his beard and hair. While thus raving, his eye turns to the fatal tree. It is as if the Satan of the mediæval mystery plays were beckoning him from its branches, saying: "Here, Judas, here is the tree; hang thyself on it quickly." He rushes towards it; gazes for a moment at the branch that seems as if made to suspend him, and tears the girdle from his garment, saying: "Ha! Come, thou serpent, entwine my neck, and strangle the betrayer." He springs at the branch; throws the end of the girdle over it; ties it about his neck; and the suicidal act is all but completed when the falling curtain hides the terrifying scene. The following monologue of Judas, which may be considered as one of the finest dramatic pieces of the play, is written by the Geistlicher Rath Daisenberger:

ACT X.—THE DESPAIR OF JUDAS.

Where can I go to hide my fearful shame?
How rid my conscience of its dreadful guilt?
No forest fastness is there dark enough!
No mountain cavern deep enough! O earth,
Ope wide thy jaws, and swallow me! I can
No longer here remain.
     Oh, my dear Master!
Him, best of all men, have I basely sold,
Giving Him up to treatment vile and rude,
Yea, perhaps to martyrdom and torture—I,
Detestable betrayer!—Is there a man
On earth on whom such guilt of blood doth
 rest?
How good the Master ever was to me!
How did He comfort me with kindly words,
When gloomy thoughts oft hover'd o'er my
 brow!
How wondrous happy did I feel when I
Sat with the brethren at His feet, and heard
Sweet, heavenly teachings from His mouth
 proceed!
How, full of love, did He admonish me,
E'en while my soul o'er scandalous treachery
Was deeply brooding,—the good Lord—
 and—
For all His goodness, have I thus repaid!

Accursed avarice! Thou alone didst lead
My heart astray: didst make me deaf and
 blind!
Thou wast the ring by which foul Satan
 held
My soul, and dragg'd me down the dread
 abyss.
No more His follower,—shall I ever dare
Before the brethren show my face again?
Shut out from them, and hated everywhere,
Despised and jeer'd, indeed, by those vile
 men
Who led me on. As a betrayer now,
Branded with shame, I wander erring on,
And bear this glowing fire within my breast!
Oh, were the Master there! Oh, could I see
His face once more! I'd cast me at His
 feet,
And cling to Him, my only saving hope!
But now He lieth in prison,—is, perhaps,
Already murder'd by His raging foe—
Alas, through my own guilt! Through my
 own guilt
I am the outcast villain who hath brought
My benefactor to these bonds and death.
The scum of men! There is no help for
 me!
For me no hope! My crime is much too
 great!
The fearful crime no penance can make
 good.
Too late! Too late! For He is dead,
 and I—
I am His murderer!
     Thrice unhappy hour,
In which my mother gave me to the world!
How long must I drag on this life of shame,
And bear these tortures in my outcast breast?
As one pest-stricken, flee the haunts of men,
And be despis'd and shunn'd by all the
 world?
Not one step further! Here, O life accursed,
Here will I end thee! On these branches
 hang
The most disastrous fruit.
 [*Undoes the girdle, and prepares to hang himself.*
     Ha! come, thou serpent,
Entwine my neck, and strangle the be-
 trayer!

Here ends the *rôle* of Iscariot. The characterization of Judas in the Passion Play differs in many essential points from the portraiture given of the betrayer by the Evangelists, who describe the deed of betrayal as the result of a sudden, malignant inspiration of a soul naturally wicked. Here the portrait is enlarged with great dramatic skill. Judas is represented to us as the incorporation of the idea "that avarice is the root of all evil." The germ of treachery sprang up at Bethany, when the costly ointment poured on the Master's feet by penitent Magdalene called up the latent avarice in Iscariot's nature. Judas had no thought of betrayal then. But fear for his future material welfare, fear that Christ was going to leave His followers unprovided for, constantly haunting his mind, prepared him to listen to the vile insinuations of the traders, and to finally accept the blood-money from the Sanhedrim. An English critic, writing in 1871, said: "The acting of Judas would be considered splendid on any stage in Europe. The naturalness and subtle rendering of the character is truly marvellous."

ACT XI.—CHRIST BEFORE PILATE.

TABLEAU. Daniel falsely accused before King Darius.—Daniel vi. 4.

THE Sanhedrim has already passed the sentence of death upon Christ. But since this body is subject to the dominion of Rome, it is necessary to get their judgment formally confirmed by Pilate, before it can be carried into execution. The introductory tableau has reference to this event: "*Scarcely,*" says the Choragus, in the opening address, "*have the words, ' He shall die!' been heard, when we hear the priests, many-tongued, hastening to the palace of Pilate, athirst with tiger-like rapacity for the blood of the Saviour. They assemble before the palace of the Gentile, impetuous, inexhaustible in abuse, bringing charge upon charge, impatiently clamouring for the sentence of condemnation. Thus, too, did a thousand voices cry out against Daniel, 'He hath destroyed Baal! Away with him to the den of lions! Let him serve them as food!' Alas, when once false illusions have effected an entrance into the human heart, the man is no longer able to command himself. Injustice groweth to be a virtue in his mind, and virtue he hateth and persecuteth!*" The Chorus sings:—

Gelästert hat er Gott!	"He hath blasphemèd God on high,
Wir brauchen keine Zeugen mehr.	What witness more have we then need?
Verdammt zum Tod	He hath deservèd death," they cry,
Ist vom Gesetze er;	"'Tis by our ancient laws decreed!"
So lärmet das Synedrium.	Thus rages wild the Council High;
Auf! zu Pilatus wollen wir,	"Up, up, to Pilate let us go!
Ihm unsre Klagen vorzubringen—	Our just demands he can't deny;
Das Todesurtheil zu erzwingen.	Death must be meted to the foe!"

TABLEAU.—The tableau shows the prophet Daniel before the throne of Darius, defending himself against his accusers. The presidents, governors, princes, councillors, and captains of the empire, we are told, had induced Darius to sign a decree, that whosoever should ask a petition of any god or man for thirty days, save of the king, should be cast into the den of lions. But Daniel continued, as was his wont, to pray to God three times every day, looking towards Jerusalem. This was his sin; and with this charge the princes and governors demanded that the monarch should sentence him to death in the den of lions. Although King Darius was sorely displeased, when he heard the charges, that he had committed himself, for he loved Daniel, he could not break his word, and was finally compelled to command that his favourite be cast into the den. The Chorus sings of the relation of this Old Testament type to the dramatic scene:—

In diesem stummen Bilde sehet ihr:	See in this scene the story told
Wie Daniel zu Babylon,	Of what took place in days of yore.
Verklagt man fälschlich Gottes Sohn.	In Daniel's fate a type behold
	Of that which is for Christ in store.

ACT XI.—CHRIST BEFORE PILATE.

Der Götter Feind ist Daniel!	The gods' great foe is Daniel.
O König! höre deiner Völker Klagen:	O King, list how thy folk complain:
Zerstört hat er den grossen Bel—	He hath destroy'd the mighty Baal,
Die Priester und den Drachen er erschlagen.	The dragon and the priesthood slain.
Ergrimmt vor deinem Thron	Enraged, before Thy throne,
Erscheint ganz Babylon.	Appears all Babylon.
Willst du von Volkes Wuth dich retten;	Wouldst thou escape the people's ire?
So lass den Feind der Götter tödten.	Then let our gods' great foe expire!
Er sterbe!—König! nur sein Tod	His death!—O King, his death alone
Versöhnet unsern groszen Gott.	Will for his wicked deeds atone.
So eilt das böse Sanhedrin	And, like these men of vile report,
Ganz rasend zu Pilatus hin,	The Council haste to Pilate's court,
Wie jene Schurken dort gethan;	And there, with raving breath,
Und klagt mit wildem Ungestüm,	Denouncing with their souls irate,
Voll Tigerwuth und Löwengrimm,	With lion's rage and tiger's hate,
Die Unschuld auf den Tod nun an.	The Innocent to death.
O Neid! satanisches Gezücht,	O envy, foulest breed of hell,
Was unternimmst, was wagst du nicht,	What darest thou not do as well
Um deinen Groll zu stillen?	Thy basest ends to gain;
Nichts ist dir heilig, nichts zu gut;	Nought is too sacred, pure, or high
Du opferst Alles deiner Wuth	Thy wickedness to satisfy;
Und deinem bösen Willen.	Nought can thy rage restrain.
Weh dem, den diese Leidenschaft	Take care, O brethren, that vile envy's
In Schlangenketten mit sich rafft!—	sway
Vor neidischen Gelüsten,	Ne'er bear you in its serpent-coils away;
O Brüder! bleibet auf der Hut!	Its sting is fatal: and its each desire
Nie lasset diese Natterbrut	Works in your heart a never-dying fire.
In euren Busen nisten!	

CHRIST BEFORE PILATE.—After the Chorus has disappeared, Christ is led before Pilate. The latter appears with his train upon the balcony of his palace. The high-priests and the Jews stand on the pavement below. They cry, "He is a blasphemer, an instigator of the people, an enemy of the emperor, for he refuses the dues, and calls himself king." Pilate knows well that this is not so, but he addresses Jesus as a judge. But Jesus does not answer. "His silence," cry the high-priests, "betrays his guilt; he has put himself up as king of the Jews." In order to prove these accusations nearer, Pilate orders Christ to be brought up to him. He then asks him, "Art thou the king of the Jews?" Christ answers dignifiedly: "My kingdom is not of this world; if my kingdom were of this world, then would my servants fight, that I should not be delivered to the Jews: but now is my kingdom not from hence . . . Thou sayest that I am a king; to this end was I born, and for this cause came I into the world, that I should bear witness unto the truth." Pilate does not understand these words relating to Christ's divine mission, and asks Jesus, "What is truth?" The course of the trial is here interrupted by one of those minor and yet significant scenes which the mediæval dramatists seldom omitted to notice, loving as they did to record all the events that might be considered supernatural, and as connected with the life of the Lord. The dream of Pilate's wife was classed in this category. The servant Quintus enters hastily upon the balcony, and informs his master that Claudius is waiting outside, bearing a message from his (Pilate's) wife. The governor orders that he be admitted, and at the same time commands the soldiers to "lead the captive, for the present, into the hall." Claudius enters and greets his master. "What message dost thou bring from my beloved wife?" Pilate asks. The servant answers: "She sends greeting to thee, and begs of thee most urgently that thou wilt have nothing to do with the just man who standeth accused before thy judgment-seat, for she hath suffered many things this day in a dream because of him." (Matt. xxvii. 19.) Though Pilate expresses his surprise at the message, it does not come unwelcome to him in his present state of mind. "Tell her," he replies, "that she need have no fear on his account. I will not submit to the Jews, but will do all in my power to rescue him."

Finally a way presents itself by which he still hopes to be relieved from further measures in relation to Christ. "Is he from Galilee?" he suddenly asks. "Yea," answer the priests, "this man is simply a Galilean." The chief rabbi adds: "He is from Nazareth, in the territory of King Herod." "Then," answers Pilate, "if that be the case, I am relieved from the office of judge. Herod hath come to Jerusalem to celebrate the feast. Let him sit in judgment over his subject. Take Him to His own king. Let Him be escorted thither by my own soldiers." Christ is now led away from the balcony. Pilate retires into his palace, glad to have placed the burden of the judgeship upon other shoulders. The priesthood linger for a moment below. Caiaphas is conscious of having gained at least a partial victory. "Up, then!" he exclaims, "let us go to Herod! We shall find at his hands better protection for our sacred laws, for he is still true to the faith of the fathers." Gesticulating and uttering violent threats and comments, the priests cross the stage, followed by the soldiers who guard the Saviour, on their way to the court of King Herod.

ACT XII.—CHRIST BEFORE KING HEROD.

TABLEAU.—Samson a sport to the Philistines.—Judges xvi.

SAMSON a sport to the Philistines: Jesus ridiculed before the court of King Herod. Such is the relation of the tableau to the dramatic scene,—of the prophecy to the fulfilment. The Choragus as usual, announces the nature of the scene to follow. "*The beloved Saviour,*" he says, "*meets with further humiliation before the court of Herod, because he refuses to flatter the monarch's vanity by exhibiting his gift of prophecy and his miraculous powers. For this reason the Most Wise is treated by fools as one like unto themselves; and as a pastime for the monarch and his hirelings, he is mockingly clothed in a white robe, and thus exhibited to public gaze. Samson, the mighty hero, feared of his enemies, was deprived of his sight, and exhibited as a bound captive by the Philistines, who ridiculed and despised him on account of his weakness. Yet, he who now seemeth to be so weak will*

ACT XII.—CHRIST BEFORE KING HEROD.

eventually prove his mightiness. He who standeth here degraded will soon glance in majesty. Virtue towereth above undeserved mockery." Before the tableau is revealed the Chorus sing :—

Vergebens sprühet vor des Richters Schranken Erboster Hass der Lästrung Flammenglut. Der Richter tritt entgegen ohne Wanken; An seiner Feste bricht der Feinde Wuth.	Embitter'd foes, their wicked ends to gain, Rage and blaspheme before the judgment-seat : Just and austere, the judge their charges meet, He stands unmoved, and all their lies are vain.
Doch ruht sie nicht ! Bekümmert gehen Wir Jesu zu Herodes nach. Dort—ach !—betrübten Herzens sehen Wir Ihm bereitet neue Schmach.	But they rest not ! Now let us sadly go, To Herod's court, where He, the Lord, is ta'en ; But who can here the flowing tears restrain, To see the treatment He must undergo ?

TABLEAU.—The story of this tableau is told in Judges xvi., how that Samson, after being betrayed by Delilah, the lords of the Philistines gathered together to offer a great sacrifice to their god Dagon, and to rejoice that Samson was in their hands. In their exultation they called for Samson to make them sport, and the strong man was set between the pillars. Samson said unto the lad that held him : "Suffer me that I may feel the pillars whereupon the house standeth, that I may lean upon them." Samson grasped them, bowed himself with all his might, and the house fell upon the lords, and all the people that were therein. The Chorus sings, in explanation :—

Seht Samson : Seht die starke Hand— Sie muss der Knechtschaft Fessel tragen! Der Held, der Tausende geschlagen— Er trägt des Sklaven Spottgewand !	See, Samson, see the mighty man, The hero of a thousand slain, The victim of a treacherous plan, Must bend beneath the bondman's chain.
Den Feinden einst so fürchterlich Dient er zu ihres Hohnes Ziele ; Philister brauchen ihn zum Spiele, Erfreu'n an seiner Schwäche sich.	'Midst foes who him could ne'er arrest He must, alas! in bondage stand ; The Philistines make him their jest, And fear no more his stalwart hand.
So steht auch Jesus, Gottes Sohn, Zu stolzer Thoren Augenweide, Geschmäht, verlacht im weissen Kleide, Und überhäuft mit Spott und Hohn.	See Jesus, too, God's only-born, Reviled, abused by foolish men ! Despised and clad in robes profane— Exposed to contempt and scorn.

CHRIST BEFORE HEROD.—The scene of Christ before Herod takes place in the central stage, generally used for the tableaux. Surrounded by his court the tetrarch sits upon an elevated golden throne. He wears a yellow velvet garment, garnished with silver and white. Priests of high standing and soldiers are present. Soon the multitude with Christ reaches the palace; but only Christ and the chief men of the escort are allowed to enter. Herod sees in the maltreated Jesus only a foolish person, hardly worth being considered as at all dangerous to the state. Christ does not answer Herod's questions, and the fat monarch's wish that Christ should perform a miracle is unheeded. He proposes all manner of things to the meek captive. "Interpret me the dream that I dreamt last night; do a miracle ; transform the roll that contains Thy death-warrant into a serpent. Thou wilt not! Thou canst not! That ought to be an easy task for thee to do." But Herod can neither get word nor deed from Christ, so, as if considering the further examination beneath his dignity, he thinks to make a laughing-stock of Him by causing a garment of ridicule to be put upon Him, a sceptre to be placed in His hand, and in this manner to be sent back to Pilate. "Clad with this magnificent royal robe," says Herod, "He will henceforth shine in His kingdom." The servant adjusts the robe, and Christ appears clad entirely in white. "Now," says Herod, "lead Him as He is before the people! They can admire their favourite as they will, till they have had enough of Him."

"Is this then thy sentence?" asks Caiaphas. "Speak the sentence of death upon Him as the law demandeth," exclaim the rest. "My sentence is," answers Herod, "that He is a fool, and not capable of the crimes which ye have laid to His charge. If He have done anything against you, then it must be attributed to His simplicity." "O king," cries Caiaphas, disappointed and enraged, "take care that thou do not err!" Herod answers, "I fear nothing. He hath done penance for His folly. The court is closed." The rabbi makes a last attempt to induce Herod to avert the "danger that threateneth the religion of Moses and the prophets." But Herod will not listen. "My word is given;" he adds, "I am tired, and will not burden myself any more with the matter. Pilate may act according to his own judgment. Bear with ye greetings and friendship from King Herod." He motions imperiously that the audience is over. The priests leave the hall in a very discontented mood, crying, "He must die! He must die! for He is the enemy of the fathers." By this time Herod himself is by no means in a pleasant humour. He had expected to derive more amusement from the captive. He descends from his throne, and, addressing himself to his courtiers, remarks: "Things have not come up to my expectation. I promised myself a most choice enjoyment, all about God knoweth what sort of wondrous tricks; and we saw simply a common-place fellow, and did not hear a sound from His lips. This man is not a John. John spake, and conversed with a wisdom and power which made one esteem him. But this man is as dumb as a fish. But come ye, my friends," he concludes, "this matter hath detained us long enough. Let us make up for lost time with music and song." The curtain falls.

ACT XIII.—THE SCOURGING AND CROWNING.

TABLEAU I. Joseph's bloody coat brought home to Jacob.—Gen. xxxvii. 32.
TABLEAU II. The ram appointed for a sacrifice in the place of Isaac.—Gen. xxii. 13.

THE spectator has followed the Saviour on His "path of sorrow" since the betrayal in Gethsemane, first to the house of the high-priest Annas, then to Caiaphas, the Sanhedrim, to Pilate's, and thence to King Herod. He now accompanies Him once more, on His return to the Roman governor. The audience is prepared for the scenes

ACT XIII.—THE SCOURGING AND CROWNING.

to follow by the address of the Choragus, which refers to the two Old Testament types that introduce them, namely, Joseph's bloody coat brought home to Jacob, and the ram appointed as sacrifice in place of Isaac. "*Alas!*" he exclaims, "*eternally lamentable is the scene presented to the gaze of Jesus' followers. The body of the Lord is covered with wounds from the countless blows of the scourge. His head is surrounded with a wreath of piercing thorns; and, overspread with bloood, His countenance is scarcely recognizable. Who can gaze on Him without that tears of the deepest sympathy roll down his cheeks? How the father Jacob trembled when he saw the coat of his favourite boy, all dripping with blood! How he wept, mourning with pain, with lamentations that pierced the heart. Let us also weep when we see the Divine Friend of our souls in pain; for, alas! it is for our sins that He is beaten and covered with wounds.*" The Chorus joins in song :—

Sie haben noch nicht ausgewüthet— Nicht ist der Rache Durst gestillt Nur über Mordgedanken brütet Die Schaar, von Satans Groll erfüllt.	Dark, murderous thoughts alone the heart engage Of this vile crew, fill'd with satanic rage; Spurr'd on by anger, for revenge athirst, They seek His death with envious tongue accursed.
Kann diese Herzen denn nichts mehr erweichen? Auch nicht ein Leib, zerfleischt von Geisselstreichen, Mit Wunden ohne Zahl bedeckt? Ist nichts, was noch ein Mitleid weckt?	Can nothing melt these harden'd hearts of vice, E'en when His body by the scourge is torn? Doth not the blood from all His wounds suffice To stay their vengeance, or appease their scorn?

TABLEAU.—The first tableau represents the story of Joseph's bloody coat brought home by the perjured brothers to their father Jacob. It is a continuation of two previous tableaux: the first, of the conspiracy among the brothers, and their resolve to cast Joseph into the well; and the second, of the sale to the Midianite merchants. Two of the brothers are holding up the bloody garment before the aged, sorrowing father. The Chorus express the paternal grief in song :—

O! welche schaudervolle Scene, Des Josephs Rock mit Blut besprengt Und an den Wangen Jakobs hängt Der tiefsten Trauer heisse Thräne.	Behold, a scene of direst woes! Young Joseph's coat, all stain'd with blood, While down good Jacob's cheeks a flood Of bitter tears of anguish flows.
Wo ift mein Joseph? meine Wonne! An dessen Aug' mein Auge ruht. An diesem Rocke hängt das Blut, Das Blut von Joseph—meinem Sohne.	"Where is my Joseph? He, my joy, On whose eye still my fond looks rest; The blood-stains darken this, his vest— The blood of Joseph—of my boy!"
Ein wildes Thier hat ihn zerrissen, Zerissen meinen Liebling. Ach! Dir will ich nach—dir, Joseph! nach; Kein Trost kann diess mein Leid versüssen:	"Some wild beast did his body rend! O, rent my darling—woe is me! Thee will I follow, Joseph, thee: No comfort can my sorrows end!"

So jammert er—so wimmert er
Um Joseph—und er ist nicht mehr.
So wird auch Jesu Leib zerrissen
  Mit wilder Wuth,
  Sein kostbar Blut
In Strömen aus den Wunden flieszen.
	Thus he laments, his heart is sore,
	For Joseph he will see no more.
	Thus, in wild rage, is torn also
	  Our Saviour good,
	  Whose precious blood
	Will from His wounds in hot streams flow!

SECOND TABLEAU.—We see to the left, and elevated, the altar upon which Isaac kneels in readiness for the sacrifice; his hands are tied behind his back, while Abraham has raised the knife to slay him. But an angel holds back Abraham's arm; and points to a ram that has got entangled in a thicket. The Chorus explains the tableau:—

Abraham! Abraham! tödt' ihn nicht.
  Dein Glaube hat—so spricht
Jehova—ihn, den Einzigen gegeben:
Er soll nun wieder dein—zum Völker-
    Glücke leben.
	"Good, Abra'm, put him not to death!
	  Thy great faith hath," Jehovah saith,
	"Given back thine only son this day
	  To be his people's guide and stay."

Und Abra'm sah im Dorngesträuch
  Verwickelt einen Widder steh'n;
Er nahm, und opferte sogleich
  Ihn, von Jehova ausersehn.
	And Abra'm in the bush espied
	  A ram entangled 'fore his eyes;
	This offering which the Lord supplied
	  He gave to Heaven as sacrifice.

Ein gross Geheimniss zeigt diess Bild Im heil'gen Dunkel noch verhüllt. Wie dieses Opfer einst auf Moria, Steht Jesus bald gekrönt mit Dörnern da.	A precious mystery doth this type contain Which must awhile in holy gloom remain, As once this victim on Moriah was found, Will Jesus stand a Victim thorn-becrown'd.

Der Dornbekrönte wird für uns sein Leben,
Wie es der Vater will, zum Opfer geben.
  Wo trifft man eine Liebe an,
  Die dieser Liebe gleichen kann?
	He, crown'd with thorns, for us His life
	    will give,
	A precious offering—that we all may live.
	  O, where find we such love as this!
	  He gives His life for others' bliss.

THE SCOURGING.—After the Chorus has retired, Christ is again brought before Pilate, who still finds Him guiltless. "By my honour," he says to the people, "I cannot find any crime in Him." But the people are not satisfied with this decision, and continually instigated by the Jewish priests, they clamour all the louder for Christ's death. Evidently Pilate wants to let Christ go if possible; he tries to appease the people, and reminds them that, as it is the custom at the feast of the Passover to give one criminal his freedom, they shall now choose between Christ and Barabbas. But the Jews are determined to have Christ put to death, and they cry out: "He must die, He is a blasphemer and a despiser of our law; crucify Him, crucify Him!" Finally Pilate wavers, and sentences the captive to be scourged, hoping thereby to appease the people.

    The scourging takes place within the central stage, where we hear the clamour and mockery of the soldiers, and, as the curtain ascends, see the last scourge-blows falling upon the back of the Saviour, who is fastened to a stake. His back is covered with blood; and as soon as He is released from the pillar, He falls senseless upon the ground. After rising again, the soldiers put on Him a scarlet (red) robe, place a sceptre in His hand, and set Him upon a stool

FIGURES FROM THE AMMERGAU THEATRE.

"MOSES."

"CHRISTUS."

ACT XIII.—THE SCOURGING AND CROWNING.

for a throne. All this in mockery. The brutality goes so far that one even pushes Him off the stool; and since His arms are bound, He falls heavily to the ground. Just as rudely do they pick Him up, and "bump" Him upon His throne again, saying, "Seat thyself, a king should not stand up." Then they bring out a crown of thorns, and amid brutal exultation, set it upon the Saviour's head, and to press it down firm, four hirelings take hold of the ends of two sticks, and thus drive the crown down over Christ's brow, the blood running over His countenance. Miss Patruban's description of this scene, written with much delicacy and tenderness of heart, may here be quoted.

She says: "It is again still on the stage. We hear cries and laughter in the distance, and the strokes of the scourge. The curtain slowly rises. What a view is revealed! Alas! the painful sight is lost in a torrent of tears! It is a room in the judgment hall of Pilate. In the foreground stands the Saviour, disrobed, bound to a pillar, bleeding, bearing the blows dealt by the unmerciful barbarians. What a heart-moving sight His form presents! Only a few strokes fall after the curtain is raised—yet each pierces our heart. A slight start at the fall of each blow, a slight tremor, the expression of pain on the countenance, the gaze directed heavenward—alone testify of what He suffers." The scene is acted as it was in the religious plays of the Middle Ages. The soldiers who scourge and abuse the Lord make use of the same doggerel verse as found in the very oldest versions of the drama. The following is an example:—

CASPIUS.

[*Putting aside the scourge.*]

Enough! Enough! Nor scourge Him more;
We've something else for Him in store.

MILO.

O Israel's king! O what a plight!
All o'er with blood! A perfect fright!
[*Laughter.*]

SABINUS.

How can He be a monarch grand?
Holds He no sceptre in His hand?
Nor doth a crown His head adorn,
As should by every king be worn;

RUSPIUS.

O wait, my friends, and I will bring
Fit gems for this, our Jewish king!

MILO.

We'll set Him out in proper style.

SABINUS.

Have patience, lord, a little while.
We are Thy servants all, and we
Will trim Thee up right royally.

CASPIUS.

[*Bringing a reed as sceptre.*]

See here, the very loveliest thing
To ornament our Jewish king!

ALL.

Ha! Ha! How grand He looks; How fine!
Knew'st not such honours could be thine?

SABINUS.

Such as we pay to Thee to-day!

CASPIUS.

[*Bringing a red mantle.*]

Now don the purple's grand array.

SABINUS.

But seat Thyself like all kings grand;
It is not seemly that Thou stand.

MILO.

[*Bringing a crown of thorns.*]

And here, a crown made wondrously:
Now let the people look at Thee!

DOMITIUS.
But set it on quite safe and sound,
Or else 'twill tumble to the ground.

MILO.

'Twere pity for such beauteous crown—
Come, fellows, help me press it down.
[*They press it down by means of two long sticks.*]

SABINUS.

The royal staff completes His store!
Now, King, Thou lackest nothing more.

CASPIUS.

How stately He appears! O see!
Our homage gracious king, to Thee!

QUINTUS.

[*Coming from the palace of Pilate.*]
Now let the prisoner be ta'en,
Before the judgment-seat again.

SABINUS.
[*To Quintus.*]
O, why disturbest thou our fun
Before our royal play is done?

MILO.
[*To Christ.*]
Arise! Now Thou wilt perhaps be led
To show the folk Thy royal head.

SABINUS.

O won't the Jews be mighty glad
To see their king so royal clad?

CASPIUS.
[*To his fellows.*]
Enough! Enough of regal sport:
Now let us take Him to the court.
[*Christ is taken into the inner court; and the curtain falls.*]

There are no mild features to the brutality of this scene, presented in its full medieval characteristics. The rude treatment of the captive is carried perhaps too far for a modern audience. On the other hand, the dignity of Christ is never allowed to suffer. The comments of visitors are of interest on this point. Speaking of the abused Saviour, when He is pushed to the ground by the hirelings, Devrient says: "He falls so as not to detract from His dignity, and the intended degradation of maltreatment reflects upon His abusers."

ACT XIV.—CHRIST SENTENCED TO DEATH.

TABLEAU I. Joseph made ruler over Egypt.—Genesis xii. 41.
TABLEAU II. The two goats as sin offerings.—Leviticus xvi. 7.

AS seen from the preceding act, whilst Christ was being scourged by Pilate's soldiers, the priests were at work inciting the people to aid them in their efforts to bring about the death of the Saviour. Pilate imagined that the scourging would fully satisfy the rage the Sanhedrim; but his mistake becomes apparent in the present act. The Choragus introduces the first scene as follows:—"*A very picture of misery the Redeemer stands before us. Even Pilate himself is moved to sympathy for Him. Hast thou still no mercy, foolish and deceived people?! No! Infatuated by the priests they cry out: 'To the cross with Him!' Nothing less than the martyrdom and death of the Saviour will satisfy them; whilst, for Barabbas the murderer, they demand pardon! O, how different did Joseph once stand before the people of Egypt! Songs of joy and gladness resounded on every side;*

ACT XIV.—CHRIST SENTENCED TO DEATH.

and he was welcomed as the deliverer of the land. But around the Saviour of the world a blinded people ceaseth not its clamour till the judge, rendered wroth, utters the sentence : ' Take Him, and crucify Him !' " The Chorus sing :—

Ach seht den König ! seht zum Hohne Gekrönt ihn ! ach, mit welcher Krone !	Behold the king ! Alas ! in rude disdain The wretches crown Him with a wreath of pain !
Und welch' ein Scepter in der Hand ! Mit Purpur seht ihr ihn behangen ; Ach ja ! im rothen Lappen prangen. Ist das des Konigs Festgewand ?	A shameful sceptre place they in His hand, In garments vile they make their victim stand ! Are these the jewels that a king should wear ? And this the treatment that the Lord must bear ?
Wo ist an ihm der Gottheit Spur ? Ach ! welch ein Mensch ! Ein Wurm—ein Spott der Henker nur.	Behold the Man ! The scoff of hangmen vile ; Thus they abuse Him, and their hours beguile.

FIRST TABLEAU.—Joseph in Egypt, raised to honour by Pharaoh. The stage is filled with a great multitude of people ; the scene is Egypt, and the pyramids are seen in the background. Upon a triumphal chariot Joseph stands, crowned with laurel wreaths ; he is magnificently clad ; a golden chain about his neck, and trumpeters announce his approach. Two slaves stand at his side to protect his countenance from the sun. The grouping of the picture can hardly be excelled. The connection of the tableau with Christ's death and resurrection to glory is well exhibited :—

Seht ! welch ein Mensch !— Zur Hoheit Joseph auserwählt Seht ! welch ein Mensch !— Zum Mitleid Jesu vorgestellt.	Behold the man ! To sovereignty young Joseph's called. Behold the man ! See, in his fate is Christ's foretold.
Laut soll es durch Aegypten schallen : Es lebe Joseph hoch und hehr ! Und tausendfach soll's wiederhallen : Aegpytens Vater—Freund ist er ! Und Alles stimme—gross und klein— In unsern frohen Jubel ein !	Loud through great Egypt's land shall sound, Long live our Joseph, good and high ; A thousand times let it resound : Great Egypt's father, friend, our cry ! And every one—whoe'er he be, Join in our festal jubilee !
Du bist Aegyptens Trost und Freude, Ein Gluck, wie ihm noch keines war. Dir, Joseph, bringt Aegypten heute Die Huldigung voll Jubel dar. Laut soll es durch Aegypten schallen, &c.	Great Egypt's trust and joy art thou, A blessing as we ne'er did see ? And Egypt bringeth, Joseph, now Its joyful homages to thee ! Loud through great Egypt's land, &c.
Als zweiter Landesvater thronet Er nun in uns'rer Mitt und Brust ! Der Herbes nur mit Segen lohnet— Ihm Heil ! des Landes Stolz und Lust. Laut soll es durch Aegypten schallen, &c.	Our country's second father, yea, Who in our hearts shall e'er abide ; The harsh with good he doth repay ; All-hail ! Our country's joy and pride ! Loud through great Egypt's land, &c.

SECOND TABLEAU.—The second tableau represents the fulfilment of the sacrifice ordained by Jehovah, as recorded in Lev. xvi. 5-21 : " And the Lord said unto Moses, speak unto Aaron thy brother. And he shall take two goats for a sin offering, and present them before the Lord at the door of the tabernacle of the congregation. And shall cast lots upon them, one lot for the Lord, and the other lot for the scapegoat. And shall bring the goat upon which the Lord's lot fell, and offer him for a sin offering. But the goat on which the lot fell to be the scapegoat, shall be presented alive before the Lord, to make an atonement with him, and to let him go for a scapegoat into the wilderness. And the goat shall bear upon him all their iniquities into a land not inhabited : and he shall let go the goat in the wilderness." The tableau is typical of the choice between Jesus and Barabbas : the latter is suffered to escape, while the former is chosen of God as an offering for the sins of the whole world. Whilst the picture is revealed the Chorus sings :—

Des alten Bundes Opfer diess,	In this, the ancient offering, see
Wie es Jehova bringen liess :	A sacrifice by God's decree :
Zwei Böcke wurden vorgestellt,	Two goats before the Lord were brought,—
Darüber dann das Loos gefällt,	The one the lot did fall upon
Wen sich Jehova, anserwählt.	By God was chosen as His own ;
Jehova, durch das Opferblut	Its blood for sinners pardon bought.
Sei deinem Volke wieder gut.	Jehovah, through the offer'd blood,
	Be to Thy people once more good.
Das Blut der Böcke will der Herr	Through blood of goats no more the Lord
Im neuen Bunde nimmermehr ;	Will e'er His precious grace afford ;
Ein neues Opfer fordert er.	He now demands an offering new,
Ein Lamm von allem Makel rein	A sacrifice of purer hue.
Muss dieses Bundes Opfer sein,	A lamb from every blemish free,
Den Eingebornen will der Herr ;	Must the new covenant's off'ring be :
Bald kommt—bald fällt—bald blutet er.	The Only Born the Lord requires :—
	He comes, He suffers, falls, expires.

Whilst the Chorus of Schutzgeister are yet upon the proscenium, one hears cries of the mob in the streets of Jerusalem. They are clamouring for the death of the Saviour, and the release of Barabbas, just as they have been instructed to do by the priesthood and their agents. They are still in the background, and while the Chorus, before the audience, pleads for the captive's life, the unseen multitude answer with fierce cries, demanding His death on the cross. This alternate singing, which forms a splendid antiphon, contrasts the fury of blind passion with the calm pleading of innocence :—

Choragus :—I hear the murderer's fearful cry:

People :—Barabbas be from fetters free !

Chorus :—No ; Jesus be from His bonds free !

Choragus :—Alas, wild cry the murderers grim !

People :—To th' cross with Him ! To th' cross with Him !

Chorus :—Ah ! look at Him the guiltless One, What evil can He e'er have done !

People :—If thou dost let this miscreant go, Then thou art our great emperor's foe !

Chorus :—Jerusalem ! Jerusalem !

Choragus :—The blood of His Son will yet the Lord avenge on you !

People :—His blood be on us, and on our children too !

Chorus :—It fall on you, and on your children too !

CHRIST SENTENCED TO DEATH.—In a previous scene Caiaphas has sent his emissaries about Jerusalem to stir up the people to clamour. The crowd

ACT XIV.—CHRIST SENTENCED TO DEATH.

makes its appearance. The priests hope to intimidate Pilate to agree to their demands. They take their stand before Pilate's house, Caiaphas and the priests, Pharisees, &c., occupying the front. Pilate has had another interview with Christ. He appears again upon his balcony, with a brilliant retinue, and again tells the Jews that he finds no guilt in Jesus. In order to arouse the sympathy of the people for the Galilean, he orders the thief Barabbas to be brought out, placed by the side of Christ, hoping thereby that the people will be induced to let Christ go, and have Barabbas put to death. A striking contrast in the two figures; Christ noble and imposing in appearance; Barabbas the picture of depravity, a man grown grey in sin. But the people cry out that Barabbas, and not Christ, shall be released. Pilate remains long steadfast; even his wife sends him word to release the Galilean; but finally, when the people threaten him with the displeasure of the emperor, he gives way to the demands of the mob, that Barabbas be released and Christ crucified. He orders water to be brought, saying, as he washes his hands, that he will not be responsible for the blood of this innocent man. "Let the two murderers who are in the prison be brought hither," he commands. "Let the chief lictor deliver them without delay to the soldiery. They have merited death—much more than the accused. The sentence of death shall be written down and publicly announced." Pilate dictates something to his secretary. While Pilate is thus engaged the soldiers emerge from the street that passes by his house, bringing with them Christ and the two malefactors. He again looks upon the scene beneath him, and says to the two malefactors: "To-day will be the end of you and your crimes. Ye shall die on the cross. Let the judgment of death now be announced." His secretary advances, and, in a loud voice, reads: "I, Pontius Pilate, lieutenant of the mighty emperor, Claudius Tiberius, in Judea, pronounce, at the importune demand of the high-priests, of the Sanhedrim, and of the whole people of Judea, the judgment of death upon a certain Jesus of Nazareth, who is accused of inciting the people to revolt, of forbidding them to pay tribute to the emperor, and of setting Himself up as King of the Jews. The same shall be nailed to the cross, and put to death, outside the walls of the city, between two malefactors, who are sentenced to death on account of a number of robberies and murders. Done at Jerusalem, on the eve of the feast of Easter." He then breaks a staff, turns quickly away from the scene, and enters the palace. "Triumph! The victory is ours," exclaims Caiaphas. "Away with Him to Golgotha," shout priests and people. "The end of the Galilean is at hand!" The mob is in motion: Caiaphas, Annas, and the priests lead them to Golgotha. The Roman soldiers follow them, escorting the condemned Saviour to Calvary. Next to these follow the two thieves, strongly guarded and roughly abused.

Christ, however, receives more humane treatment at the hands of Pilate's soldiers than He did from the guard of the Temple. Even in this apparently unimportant detail the Ammergauers have made a clear distinction, connecting mere recruits with the Synagogue, whilst soldier-like men are placed under command of Pilate's centurion. A multitude of the people of Jerusalem closes the procession. Thus is the dreadful end brought about; thus, as

Devrient has well expressed it, is the Ideal of all that is human fairly pushed out of existence by this surging of passion, infatuation, and miserable fickleness.

ACT XV.—CHRIST BEARS HIS CROSS TO GOLGOTHA.

TABLEAU   I. Young Isaac bears the altar-wood up Mount Moriah.—Genesis xxii.
TABLEAU II. The Children of Israel bitten by the fiery serpents.—Numbers xxi. 6.
TABLEAU III. The Israelites look on the brazen serpent and are healed.—Num. xxi. 9.

THE tragedy of Golgotha has a sad prelude in the spectacle of Christ bearing His cross to the place of crucifixion. This scene is introduced by three prophetic types, thus briefly explained. As young Isaac once carried the wood up Mount Moriah for the altar whereon he was to have been sacrificed, so Christ bears His own cross up the rugged way to Golgotha. As once the children of Israel suffered from the bites of the fiery serpents till Moses raised the brazen serpent for the people to look upon and be healed, so humanity is tortured by the fiery serpents of sin, until the Redeemer is raised up on the cross, and all who look to Him and believe are healed. Says the Choragus: " *The sentence of death wrung from Pilate is pronounced. We see Jesus bowed down by the cross, staggering to the place of skulls. Isaac once bore willingly up the mountain-side the wood for the sacrifice, when he himself was to be the offering, acceding to the will of Jehovah. Jesus, too, willingly bears the burden of the cross, which will become a source of blessing and a tree of life through the sacrifice of His sacred body upon it. For as the brazen serpent which Moses lifted up in the desert brought healing to the children of Israel, so from the tree of the cross will proceed for us blessing and salvation.*" The Chorus sings, introducing the tableaux,—

Betet an und habet Dank!	Give prayer and thanks with every breath,
Der den Kelch der Leiden trank,	For He who paths of sorrow trod
Geht nun in den Kreuzestod	Goes now on to His bitter death,
Und versöhnt die Welt mit Gott.	To reconcile the world with God.

FIRST TABLEAU.—Isaac is seen bearing the wood up the heights of Moriah. Abraham is walking by his side. The Chorus sings:—

Wie das Opferholz getragen	As Isaac bore the altar wood
Isaak selbst auf Moria,	Up to the mount at Abra'm's hest;
Wanket, mit dem Kreuz beladen,	On Calvary's hill the Saviour good
Jesus hin nach Golgotha.	Is with the cross's load oppress'd.
Betet an und habet Dank, &c.	Thank the Lord with every breath, &c.

SECOND TABLEAU.—Moses elevates the brazen serpent upon a cross. If the palm of beauty must be given to the tableau of the rain of manna, the merit of skill in portraying misery must be accorded to the second of these three tableaux, in which three hundred persons take part.

ACT XV.—CHRIST BEARS HIS CROSS TO GOLGOTHA.

Angenagelt wird erhöhet	Nail'd and bruisèd they will raise
An dem Kreuz der Menschensohn,	The Son of Man on th' cross on high ;
Hier an Moses Schlange sehet,	On Moses' brazen serpent gaze,
Ihr des Kreuzes Vorbild schon.	It doth that cross well typify.
Betet an und habet Dank, &c.	Thank the Lord with every breath, &c.

THIRD TABLEAU.—The brazen serpent again. Moses stands near it, pointing to it. Besides him stands Aaron. The Children of Israel all around; those bitten by the fiery serpents look upon the brazen one, and are healed. The Chorus sings:—

Von den gift'gen Schlangenbissen	Thereby from fiery serpents' sting
Ward dadurch das Volk befreit !	God did His chosen people heal,
So wird von dem Kreuze fliessen	The cross of Christ to us will bring
Auf uns Heil und Seligkeit.	All-heavenly bliss and grace and weal.
Betet an und habet Dank, &c.	Thank the Lord with every breath, &c.

CHRIST BEARING THE CROSS.—From the gateway by the side of Pilate's palace emerges a small group of men and women, walking slowly toward the centre of the proscenium. Deep gloom overshadows their countenances. This is especially true of Mary, the mother of Christ, who is the central figure of the group. She is accompanied by the disciple John, Joseph of Arimathea, Mary Magdalene, and other women, who have come to Jerusalem, to search for Christ, and to find out what the priests have done with Him. Suddenly tumultuous cries are heard in the streets of Jerusalem. The searching group become alarmed. "What is that? A fearful noise!" exclaims Joseph of Arimathea. "As of a thousand voices!" adds a frightened maid-servant. Looking down the street that passes by the palace of Annas, the audience learns the cause of the alarm, although Mary and her friends cannot as yet perceive it. Christ is bearing His cross to Golgotha. At first only a fraction of the mob appears, shouting : "Away with Him ! He must die !" Another incident now attracts the attention of the spectators. The curtain of the central stage has been raised, and the audience looks along another street of Jerusalem, away down which is seen a strong, robust figure, clad in plain costume, and bearing on his arm a carpenter's basket. It is Simon of Cyrene.

An incident of interest is here interwoven. We refer to the alleged biblical origin of the legend of Ahasuerus, the Wandering Jew, who has become the symbol of the Jewish people in their wanderings over the face of the globe. At the very last house before the gateway, Christ, exhausted by the burthen of the cross, would fain rest. But the door of the house suddenly opens, and there appears a small, deformed specimen of humanity, whose features are stamped with maliciousness. "Away from my house ;" he cries out at the Saviour, "here is no place for Thee to rest !" Christ gazes on the speaker without uttering a word ; but His silence and look are significant of that curse which legend has ever attached to the Wandering Jew. In earlier Passion Plays this scene of Ahasuerus driving the Saviour away from his door had much more scope given it, as is shown by the following verses from a mediæval manuscript :—

THE PASSION PLAY.

AHASUERUS.

Away, thou Nazarene, away;
Here is no place for Thee to stay!

CHRIST.

I'll rest Me here a little while;
But thou shalt be a grim exile,
To roam the world, struck by the curse.
And though thou never need'st of purse,
Nor garments tear by storm or wind,
Salvation thou shalt never find.
And where thou art shalt find no rest,
Since thou didst not heed My request;
Nor shall death touch thy hoary head
Until I come to judge the dead.

The entire procession has gradually come into full view. It is headed by a Roman horseman, carrying the national standard, on which is read, "S. P. Q. R." (*Senatus Populusque Romanus*). Then comes a centurion with a company of soldiers, the immediate escort of the condemned Saviour, who, still wearing the crown of thorns, bears the weight of His ponderous cross. He is the central figure of the group, to which all eyes are attracted. He moves slowly, staggering at every step, and, to all appearance, utterly exhausted. But behind are His executioners, urging Him on by blows and pushes, while the priests and the rabble attempt to accelerate His steps by loud and jeering cries. Next to the executioners follow the two thieves condemned to be crucified with Christ, bearing crosses of a lighter construction than the Saviour's. More soldiers, and the boisterous priesthood, led by Caiaphas, Annas, and some of the prominent members of the Sanhedrim, follow, and a great crowd of the people of Jerusalem, making at least five hundred persons now before the spectator. The painfulness of the scene is increased by the slow movement of the cortège, caused by the weakness of the condemned, who, at last, completely exhausted, His countenance covered with blood, is unable to proceed even under the goading of the executioners. He staggers, and, borne down by the cross, falls heavily to the ground. On the opposite side of the proscenium stand Mary and her friends. The next moment reveals to them the fearful reality as to Who is being taken to death.

The mother is the first to discover the cruel fact. "It is He," she exclaims. "God, my God! It is my son! It is my Jesus!" Unable to bear the excitement, she sinks back into the arms of her attendants. Jesus falls exhausted, to the vexation of the executioners, who long to be at their work, and to the mortification of the priesthood. The Roman centurion shows a more humane disposition. He motions to the executioners to desist, and, handing Christ a flagon, says: "Here, refresh Thyself!" Jesus tries to rise, but cannot. The priests and Pharisees are incensed at the delay, which might be still greater, were not Simon of Cyrene espied by the chief rabbi. They remove the heavy cross from Christ, and place it upon the carpenter. A ray of joy seems to glide over the features of the new captive as he feels the weight of the cross. "Oh," he exclaims, "out of love to Thee will I bear it. Would that I could be of service to Thee!" "The blessing of God be upon thee and thine," is Christ's answer and thanks. The centurion commands that the cortège be again set in motion. The procession moves on, but not fast enough for the executioners and priests. "Now," one of the former says to Christ, "Thou canst move Thy feet a little quicker." Another would abuse

ACT XV.—CHRIST BEARS HIS CROSS TO GOLGOTHA.

Him; but the centurion bids him, "Cease! All goeth well now. We will rest here awhile. The Man needeth a short respite before He ascendeth the hill of death." "What! More delay?" exclaims Caiaphas, irritated at the many hindrances in reaching the place of execution.

While the procession is resting another scene occupies the attention of the audience. From the street in the central stage a number of women of Jerusalem appear, weeping at the Saviour's fate. Among them is the legendary Veronica, who, advancing towards Christ, says: "O Lord! Thy countenance is all covered with sweat and blood! Wilt Thou not take this," handing Him a linen-cloth, "to wipe Thyself!" He takes the cloth, presses it to His face, and returns it to Veronica, who finds upon it the imprint of the Redeemer's features. [This scene was omitted in the later performances of the year 1871, on account of its legendary character, and, perhaps, in order not to give offence to other creeds.] Christ turns towards the women, and saying: "Daughters of Jerusalem! Weep not for Me, but weep for yourselves, and for your children. For, behold, the days are coming, in the which they shall say, Blessed are the barren, and the wombs that never bare, and the breasts that never gave suck. Then shall they begin to say to the mountains, Fall on us; and to the hills, Cover us! For if they do these things in a green tree, what shall be done in the dry." "Remove now these women-folk," commands the centurion. And the executioner rudely obeys the order. The procession is again in motion, and slowly the cortège of death passes away.

On the opposite side of the proscenium the little group about Mary still remains. The mother is supported by Magdalene and the other women. She has seen her Son. The Son has seen His mother; but no words of greeting have passed between them, though tears have not alone flowed from Mary's eyes. The procession is now entirely out of sight. It is at this juncture that John says to Mary: "Come, beloved mother, let us return to Bethany. Thou wilt not be able to bear the sight!" She, true to her maternal instinct, responds: "Can a mother part from her child in the time of danger—of bitterest need? I will suffer with Him, I will share His elevation and degradation; will die with Him. I have prayed to God for strength," she answers. "The Lord hath heard me. We will follow!" "Mother," say all the members of the little group, "we follow thee."

ACT XVI.—THE CRUCIFIXION.

Three crosses in the noon-day night uplifted,
Three human figures, that in mortal pain,
Gleam white against the supernatural darkness!
Two thieves that writhe in torture, and between them
The suffering Messiah, the Son of Joseph,
Ay, the Messiah Triumphant, Son of David!

A crown of thorns on that dishonour'd head!
Those hands that heal'd the sick, now pierced with nails,
Those feet that wander'd homeless through the world
Now cross'd and bleeding, and at rest for ever.

Longfellow.

HE climax of the Ammergau drama is reached. On all previous occasions the Chorus of Schutzgeister have appeared on the proscenium, clad in their rainbow-coloured robes. In the first acts their countenances beamed with joy for the glad tidings they had to impart. In the present act, however, they have ceased to rejoice, and have donned the garb of mourning, as an expression of their sorrow for the Lamb that is taken to the slaughter. Slowly they take their accustomed places before the audience, when the Choragus addresses to the spectators the following verses, accompanied by soft, sad music, while the whole band joins in the concluding chorus:—

Auf, fromme Seelen, auf und gehet
Von Reue, Schmerz und Dank durchglüht,
Mit mir zu Golgatha, und sehet,
Was hier zu eurem Heil geschieht.
　Dort stirbt der Mittler zwischen Gott
　Und Sünder den Vermittlungstod.

Ach! nackt, von Wunden nur bekleidet,
Liegt er hier bald am Kreuz für dich;
Die Rache der Gottlosen weidet
An seiner Blösse frevelnd sich,
　Und er, der dich, o Sünder, liebt,
　Schweigt, leidet, duldet und vergibt.

Ich hör' schon seine Glieder krachen,
Die man aus den Gelenken zerrt,
Wem soll's das Herz nicht beben machen,
Wenn er den Streich des Hammers hört,
　Der schmetternd, ach! durch Hand und Fusz,
　Grausame Nägel treiben musz.

Arise, ye pious souls, and come,
While penitence your hearts inspire,
With me, and see, 'mid Calvary's gloom,
What for your saving doth transpire:
　There, for your sins, the Lord doth give
　His life that all the world may live.

See, naked, and with wounds all o'er
He suffers on the cross for thee;
On Him the godless insult pour,
And gloat upon His misery.
　And He who loves each one that lives,
　Is silent, suffers, and—forgives.

I hear His tender limbs give way
As they from out their joints are broke;
Whose heart fills not with dread dismay
When he now hears the hammer's stroke,
　Which, through His precious hands and feet
　The large and painful nails must beat.

During these words heavy hammer-blows are heard behind the scenes. The executioners are nailing Christ to the cross. The Choragus continues, as the curtain ascends:—

Auf, fromme Seelen! naht dem Lamme
Das sich für euch freiwillig schenkt.
Betrachtet es am Kreuzesstamme:
Seht, zwischen Mörder aufgehängt
Gibt Gottes Sohn sein Blut, und ihr—
Gebt keine Thräne ihm dafür?

Come, pious souls, the Lamb draw nigh,
Who gives His life so willingly;
Upon the cross suspended high
Between two malefactors, see,
　God's Son His sacred blood doth shed.
　And ye? Have ye no tears instead?

ACT XVI.—THE CRUCIFIXION.

Selbst seinen Mördern zu vergeben,	Yea, e'en His murderers to forgive,
Hört man ihn gleich zum Vater fleh'n,	We hear Him pray with dying breath;
Und bald, bald endigt er sein Leben,	Soon He for us His life will give
Damit wir ew'gem Tod entgeh'n.	To free us from eternal death.
Durch seine Seite dringt ein Speer	Yea, through His side the spear doth bore,
Und öffnet uns sein Herz noch mehr.	And opens up His heart still more.

The Choragus sings, joined in the last four lines by the whole Chorus:—

Wer kann die hohe Liebe fassen,	Who can such love as His conceive,
Die bis zum Tode liebt,,	That loveth unto death;
Und statt der Mörder Schaar zu hassen,	Who 'stead of hating can forgive
Noch segnend ihr vergibt.	His foes with dying breath!
O bringet dieser Liebe	O bring as offering to this love
Nur fromme Herzenstriebe	The thanks that every heart should move;
Am Kreuzaltar	And lay it, while the Saviour dies,
Zum Opfer dar.	Before the cross as sacrifice.

THE CRUCIFIXION.—The Schutzgeister retire from the proscenium, and the rising curtain reveals the scene on Calvary, the most intense portraiture of the entire drama. The two malefactors already hang on their crosses. On the ground, with the head slightly elevated, is a larger cross on which the Saviour is nailed. An executioner takes the inscription and nails it to the cross, above the head of Christ; and then he calls his companions, who raise the cross to an upright position. The participants in the scene take up their position in front and at either side of the crosses, while many of Christ's near friends are seen in the distant background. The Roman soldiers take up their position in line to the right of the scene; the priests and Pharisees stand at the left. Many of the Jewish people are among the lookers-on. The scene of the "three crosses in the noon-day night uplifted" is one producing the most incomprehensible feelings in the heart of the spectator. He gazes on the scene in deep amazement, doubting for the moment whether it is the reality or acting that he is witnessing. "Are we not," asks Devrient, "transported back more than eighteen hundred years to the hill of Calvary, outside the walls of Jerusalem?" The figure of Christ is the object on which all eyes centre. The two thieves are simply tied to their crosses, having their arms thrown back over those of the crosses for support. Christ, however, is placed upon His cross in a manner corresponding to the reality; His arms are stretched at full length and His hands and feet apparently pierced with nails; His whole form and countenance express the severest torture; and, as remarked, it is difficult to believe He is not actually nailed to the cross, as no trace of any ligament can be discerned. The impression created is intensely affecting.

The priests are overjoyed at the result they have at last attained, until they perceive the inscription on the cross, "THIS IS JESUS OF NAZARETH, THE KING OF THE JEWS!" Caiaphas is incensed at the insult; and sends messengers to Pilate, demanding that the inscription be changed to the words, "I am the King of the Jews!" Caiaphas, determined to know for a certainty that the enemy of the Synagogue is dead, bids them likewise: "Request Pilate to command that the limbs of the crucified be broken, and that the bodies be taken down from the crosses before the eve of the feast." The messengers soon return with a refusal. "What I have caused to be written remaineth written," is Pilate's reply to their request. As to the breaking of the limbs, about which Caiaphas is very anxious, Pilate tells the messengers that his servants will receive the necessary orders.

The minutest incident connected with the crucifixion is carried out as mentioned in the Gospel narrative, even to the casting of lots for the Saviour's garments by the executioners, as recorded by St. Mark. The priests and the mob do not cease to ridicule their foe, though he is nailed to the cross. The priest Joshua ironically looks up at Christ, and reads the inscription: "'King of the Jews?' Ah! If thou art the king in Israel, descend now from the cross, so that we may see and believe." "He saved others," says Caiaphas, "Himself He cannot save." Annas exclaims: "He trusted in God: let Him deliver Him now, if He will have Him: for He said, 'I am the Son of God!'" "Father forgive them, for they know not what they do!" is the Redeemer's prayer for His remorseless enemies. The thief on the left of the Crucified calls out in rude tones to Him: "Yea, if thou be the Christ save thyself and us!" But the other malefactor believes on the Lord, and cries out, "Lord, remember me when thou comest into Thy kingdom!" And Christ looks tenderly upon the repentant man, saying: "Verily I say unto thee, to-day thou shalt be with me in Paradise!" To the audience the scene is of painful interest. Christ has already been several minutes on the cross, and the spectators feel that the crucified before them cannot possibly remain longer in his position. The sobs of the audience mingle with those of the players.

Back of the cross, stands Mary, surrounded by her friends, all weeping bitterly. They wish to approach the scene of agony, and the Roman centurion commands that the space about the foot of the cross be cleared for the friends and relatives of the crucified. The soldiers do his bidding, and the priests retire somewhat, murmuring loudly, and Mary and her friends come forward. Mary Magdalene stands near the foot; a little to the right is the Virgin. Behind her are Joseph of Arimathea, the venerable Nicodemus, and the apostle John—the only disciple present. Lazarus stands to the left. The other men and women of the little band stand in groups with those of Jerusalem. Christ looks down upon His mother and upon the beloved disciple with a gaze of indescribable tenderness, and says: "Woman, behold thy son!" And to John: "Son, behold thy mother!" "After this," St. John relates, " Jesus knowing that all things were now accomplished, that the Scriptures might be fulfilled, saith, I thirst!" "He is athirst," says the centurion, "and calleth for water." He commands that the cravings of the Sufferer be satisfied. "And they filled a sponge with vinegar, and put it upon hyssop, and put it to His mouth." But the sponge has barely touched Christ's lips before He raises His eyes suddenly to Heaven, and cries aloud, " Eli, Eli, lama sabachthani—My God, my God, why hast Thou forsaken me?" "What doth He mean?" ask two of the Pharisees. "He calleth for Elias," replies another. "Let us see if Elias will come to take Him down," ironically

ACT XVI.—THE CRUCIFIXION.

exclaims Caiaphas. The end approaches. The convulsive movements that agitate the body announce dissolution. He again lifts up His countenance and cries with a loud voice, "It is finished! O Father! Into thy hands I commend my spirit." The Saviour's head sinks heavily upon His breast. The body is motionless. The struggle is over!

But at the same time the elements of nature are unloosed. The earth quakes, the thunder rolls, and darkness spreads over the scene. Indescribable fear seizes the Jewish spectators. The Roman centurion, awed by the supernatural events, exclaims: "Truly this was a righteous man! Truly He is the Son of God." A servant of the Temple rushes in and announces that the curtain of the Sanctuary is rent in twain." Even the priesthood are not free from fear, although Caiaphas would attribute the phenomena to the agency of Beelzebub rather than to Jehovah. "Let us go," Caiaphas adds, "and see what hath taken place! But I will immediately return, for I cannot rest until I have seen the limbs broken, and the bodies cast into the deep grave of malefactors." Caiaphas is once more doomed to have His plans thwarted. The executioners have orders to break the limbs of the crucified; an action done somewhat imperfectly. Christ being already dead, His corpse is spared by the centurion, who, however, to make sure that the Saviour is dead, pierces His side with his lance. The executioners take down the two thieves from the cross, and are about to take down the body of Christ, when Joseph of Arimathea appears with the permission from Pilate to take the corpse away and bury it. The executioners and soldiers then retire, leaving Nicodemus, Joseph of Arimathea, John, and the women to do the work of love.

THE DESCENT FROM THE CROSS.—The scene of the descent from the cross is one demanding peculiar skill and patience on the part of all engaged in it. Christ has already been suspended upon the cross over twenty minutes; His limbs are stiffened, and He has to be moved with the tenderest care. The women stand about the cross, and look on as the men proceed to take down the body. Mary, exhausted by grief, seats herself on a rock near by. The scene, as a whole, is copied from Rubens' celebrated picture, though it differs from the latter in many details. The action is done with delicacy of feeling and tenderness peculiar to all that the Ammergauers have to do in connection with Christ. Two ladders are placed against the cross; a short one at the front, and another at the back reaching to its full height. Joseph of Arimathea mounts the one in front, holding in his hand a roll of linen-cloth rolled in from both ends. Nicodemus has ascended the ladder at the back of the cross. Joseph of Arimathea reaches one end of the linen-cloth, after passing it under the left arm of the crucified. Nicodemus passes it over the left arm of the cross, and then lets it fall to the ground. Joseph passes the other end under the right arm, and Nicodemus allows it to fall over the cross to the ground. Simon of Bethany now holds one end, and a servant of Joseph of Arimathea, who is to prevent the body from falling, holds the other. Nicodemus then tenderly takes the crown of thorns from the Saviour's head, and reaches it to a servant, who places it at the feet of the mother. He then draws out the nails from the hands, and in a moment one arm is freed, and taken by Joseph of Arimathea upon his shoulder. The other arm is released by Nicodemus, and received by Joseph of Arimathea in the same manner, so that the body now rests entirely upon the latter's shoulders, at the same time that it is supported by the cloth. "O come, thou precious, sacred burthen!" exclaims Joseph, as he feels the weight of the corpse upon him. "Come upon my shoulders!" The feet are still fastened to the cross; and whilst Joseph bears up the body, Nicodemus draws out the nails. John takes the feet of the body, and Lazarus reaches up his arms to receive it, saying: "Come, sacred body of the dearest friend! Let me embrace Thee! O how hath the rage of the foe maltreated Thee!" The linen is removed, and the body, which is tenderly and reverently borne away by the four, Nicodemus, Joseph, John, and Lazarus, and laid with great care upon a white linen-cloth which the servants have spread before the mother, who takes the Saviour's head in her hands. "O my son," exclaims the weeping woman, as she bends over the dead, "how covered with wounds is Thy body." John comforts her with these words: "Mother, from these wounds flowed the fulness of blessing for all mankind." Mary Magdalene kneels at the left side of the body. The anointing of the body is then performed. The body is then wrapped in the linen-cloth, and the four men bear it away to the sepulchre, followed by the sorrowing women. In the background is seen the garden. In the centre is a huge rock, wherein the tomb has been hewn. The corpse is laid in its resting-place with no other services than these simple words: "Friend, rest in peace in the sepulchre!" "Let us now retire," says John. "Come, beloved mother"—John, Mary, and the women leave the garden, slowly, whilst Joseph of Arimathea and Nicodemus remain behind to place the stone before the door of the sepulchre. "After the festival," Nicodemus remarks, "we will complete our labour of love!" "Friend," responds Joseph, "let us lament the death of the Beloved!" And Nicodemus replies:—

"O this good man, so full of truth and grace,
How did he then deserve so sad a fate!"

ACT XVII.—THE RESURRECTION.

TABLEAU I. Jonas cast on dry land by the whale.—Jonah ii. 10.
TABLEAU II. The Israelites cross the Red Sea in safety.—Exodus xiv.

THE Passion drama does not conclude with Golgotha. The scene of the resurrection is prefigured by two Old Testament tableaux: the prophet Jonah cast on dry land by the fish, a type alluded to by Christ Himself in speaking of His resurrection. The second represents the Israelites led safely by Moses across the Red Sea, whilst the waters engulph the pursuing hosts of Pharaoh. The Chorus of Schutzgeister appear once more. They have laid aside their mourning, donned their apparel of rainbow hues, and assumed their usual joyousness. The Choragus delivers

ACT XVII.—THE RESURRECTION.

his address, in which he refers to the connection of type and fulfilment, and concludes with words expressive of the hope that all present may finally unite around the throne of Him whose sufferings, death, and glorification have been the subject of the concluding dramatic labours. *"All is finished!"* he says. *" Peace and joy are ours. His conflict hath brought us freedom; His death hath brought us life eternal! Oh, the heart of the redeemed should be inspired with gratitude and love to the Redeemer. Lowered into the tomb the Saviour rests; but it is only a brief repose. The body of the Anointed will not be touched by decay; but will again rise with renewed life. Jonah, the prophet, came out of the belly of the whale after three days. Israel passed victoriously through the waves of the Red Sea, while the pursuing foe was destroyed. Thus will the Lord rend with His might the portal of the tomb; from the gloom of night He will rise in glory, beaming with light, to the consternation of His enemies. Let the sight of the Risen One inspire your hearts with joy and hope. Return to your homes, O friends, filled with the tenderest love for Him who loved you even unto death, who still loveth you, and will love you eternally in Heaven. About His celestial throne resoundeth the eternal song of this victory, 'Praise to the Lamb, who for the world was slain!' There, united about the Saviour, we shall all see each other again."* The Chorus join with the Choragus in the following chant:—

Liebe! Liebe! In dem Blute
Kämpftest Du mit Gottes Muthe
  Deinen grossen Kampf hinaus.
Liebe! Du gabst selbst das Leben
  Für uns Sünder willig hin:
Stets soll uns vor Augen schweben
  Deiner Liebe hoher Sinn.

Ruhe sanft nun, heil'ge Hülle,
In des Felsengrabes Stille
  Von den heissen Leiden aus!
Ruhe sanft im Schooss der Erde,
  Bis Du wirst verkläret sein.
Der Verwesung Moder werde
  Nie Dein heiliges Gebein.

Oh, Love divine! With godlike migh
That fought, in flesh, the bitter fight,
  Unto the bitter end!
Oh, Love, that willingly did give
  Its life that sinners all might live,
  And grace for them obtain'd:
For evermore before our eyes
Shall rise this glorious sacrifice.

Now rest, O sacred frame, O rest,
Within the silent earth's calm breast,
  Thy sufferings all o'er;
Released from all terrestrial pain,
Rest until Thou, on Calvary slain,
  Shalt rise to life once more.
For foul decay will ne'er betide
Thy sacred body crucified.

FIRST TABLEAU.—The resurrection of Christ is prefigured in the picture of the prophet Jonah being cast by the whale upon dry land. In the background of the central stage we see the troubled sea, upon which a boat sails. Jonah is seen just stepping out of the whale's mouth upon the dry land. The Chorus sings:—

Wie Jonas in des Fisches Bauche—
  So ruhet in der Erde Schooss
Des Menschen Sohn.—Mit einem Hauche
  Reisst Bande er und Siegel los.

Triumph! Triumph! Er wird ersteh'n.
  Wie Jonas aus des Fisches Bauch,
So wird der Sohn des Menschen auch
Neu lebend aus dem Grabe geh'n.

As Jonah once within the whale—
  So rests within the earth's great womb
The Son of Man—He rends the veil,
  The bonds and seals about His tomb!

Triumph! Triumph! He will arise!
  As Jonah from the fish's maw,
So Christ the Son will rise also,
From out the grave, where now He lies.

SECOND TABLEAU.—The children of Israel have already crossed the Red Sea in safety. The hosts of Pharaoh attempt to follow them, but the waves have closed in, and engulphed them. The scene is well represented; between the surging waves we see the drowning warriors, the sinking chariots, &c. Moses and the children of Israel stand upon the banks, looking on the scene. Like as the Israelites came saved from amid the waves, so will Christ come forth as victor through death and the grave, while His enemies will be destroyed. The Chorus sings:—

Gross ist der Herr! Gross seine Güte!	The Lord is great! the Lord is good!
Er nahm sich seines Volkes an.	He made Himself His people's stay.
Er führte durch der Wogen Mitte	He once led Israel through the flood
Einst Israel auf trockner Bahn.	Through dangers great, on solid way.
Triumph, der todt war, wird ersteh'n;	Oh, triumph! He who died will rise;
Ihn decket nicht des Todes Nacht.	No power o'er Him has death's dark night,
Neu lebend wird aus eigner Macht.	New living by His own great might,
Der Sieger aus dem Grabe geh'n.	As Victor from the grave He'll rise!

THE RESURRECTION.—The ascending curtain reveals four soldiers watching at the closed and sealed grave; they are speaking with one another about the fearful phenomena connected with the crucifixion. Finally, they fall asleep. Suddenly an earthquake is felt; the stone falls from before the sepulchre, and Christ rises majestically from the grave, steps out, and disappears. The soldiers are dumb with terror, but after some time gather up courage enough to examine the grave, and find that the occupant has disappeared. Then come a number of the women, bearing costly ointment, wherewith to embalm the body; but they, too, find it no more. Entering the garden, they express fears about being able to remove the large stone from before the grave; but they find it already fallen, and their sadness increases when they cannot find the Master. An angel appears from the depth of the grave, and tells them that they should go to Galilee, where they would find the arisen One. Soon, too, come the Pharisees, and let the watchers tell them all they know about the event. They offer money to induce the soldiers to lie, and to say, "While we slept the disciples came and took away His body." The soldiers refuse at first to do this, fearing punishment; but the Pharisees promise that they will prevent any punishment. One of the soldiers remains steadfast, however, saying: "By my honour, I will relate it just as it took place."

Then comes the scene in which Christ appears to Mary Magdalene, who is lamenting the loss of her Lord and Master, and is seeking Him. She reclines against the sepulchre, when Jesus appears before her, though she does not know it. He addresses her, "Woman, why weepest thou? Whom seekest thou?" And Mary, without lifting her eyes, and thinking that it is the gardener who has spoken, replies: "O master if thou hast taken Him away, then tell me where thou hast laid Him, that I may once more ——" "Mary!" answers the mysterious form, with a gentle voice. That single word enables her to recognize Him. She leaps for joy, and cries: "O that is

ACT XVIII.—THE ASCENSION.

His voice!" She hastens towards Him, and throws herself at His feet to embrace them, as she exclaims: "Rabboni!" "Touch me not," says Christ, "for I am not yet ascended to my Father; but go to my brethren, and say unto them, I ascend unto my Father, and your Father, and to my God and your God." "Beloved Teacher!" she replies, bowing her head to the ground. When she looks up again, He has disappeared. She, however, knows that she has seen Him, her beloved Redeemer, and, full of joy, says:—

" But I have seen His face,
Have heard His voice! O moment this of bliss!
Away all sorrows and all darksome fears!
My soul is fill'd with joys of Paradise!
Now I will hasten, as though borne aloft,
And to the brethren as on wings will speed,
And bear the message He hath given to me.
Tell them the Lord is now among the living!

O, could I cry aloud through all the world,
So that the mountains, valleys, rocks, and woods,
And Heaven and earth give back their echoes:
Hallelujah! He is risen!"
[*Echo from all sides.*
" Hallelujah! He is risen!"

ACT XVIII.—THE ASCENSION.

"HE is risen!" The Chorus enter upon the proscenium for the last time, to announce the glad tidings of the event witnessed in the preceding act. "*He is risen!*" says the Choragus, his face beaming with joy as he delivers his last message to the assembled thousands of spectators. "*Sing and be glad, ye heavenly hosts! He is risen! Sing and be glad, ye mortals on earth! The scion from the house of Judah hath crushed the head of the serpent. Our faith is firmly established. Most blissful hopes are awakened in our breasts by the type and pledge of our own future resurrection! Sing in exultant tones:* '*Hallelujah!*' *We saw him enter Jerusalem, full of meekness, alas, to meet with the deepest humiliation. Now, let us gaze, before we separate, upon the triumphant festival of victory! Behold Him as He ascends to the highest glory. Full of heavenly majesty He enters the New Jerusalem, where He will gather together all those whom He hath purchased with His Blood.*" The entire Chorus joins in a joyous hymn of praise and victory, which introduces the closing tableau—the Ascension:—

Hallelujah!
Ueberwunden—überwunden
Hat der Held der Feinde Macht.
Er—er schlummerte nur Stunden
In der düstern Grabesnacht.
Singet Ihm in heil'gen Psalmen!
Streuet Ihm des Sieges Palmen!
Auferstanden ist der Herr!
Iauchzet Ihm, ihr Himmel zu!
Sing' dem Sieger, Erde du!
Halleluja Dir Erstandner!

Hallelujah!
Hallelujah! now victorious,
Breaks the Lord the hostile might!
He the Hero great and glorious
Lifts the grave's sad gloom of night!
In thrilling psalm of joy adore Him,
Strew the victor's palms before Him,—
For the Lord is now arisen!
Praise Him in song ye Heavens above!
Praise Him all ye on earth that move!
Hallelujah! He is risen!

THE ASCENSION.—Still singing its song of praise and victory, the Chorus retire a few paces, in order to direct the gaze of the audience to the tableau now revealed in the central stage. In the middle of a company of his friends and disciples, the risen Christ, clad in the same brilliant apparel with which He rose from the grave, stands on the brow of Olivet, holding in His left hand a banner emblematical of victory, whilst His right hand is raised as if to bless those who bow at His feet or stand about Him as witnesses of His glorious ascension. On either side of Him, and pointing to His person, are the two angelic figures mentioned in the Acts of the Apostles (i. 11), who said to the witnesses: "Ye men of Galilee, why stand ye gazing up into heaven? This same Jesus, which is taken up from you into heaven, shall so come in like manner as ye have seen Him go into heaven." Kneeling at the foot of the elevation upon which Christ stands are children-genii, the Adorers of the Cross; while still further in front, to the right of the Lord, kneeling, with hands folded on her breast, is Mary, the mother of the Lord. To his right and left are seen the well-known figures of the apostles, John, shading his eyes as he watches the disappearing form of the Master, with Peter at his side, together with those friends of the Lord who comforted Him at Bethany—Martha, Mary Magdalene, Simon and Lazarus; the women of Jerusalem who bewailed his fate as He bore His cross to Golgotha; also Veronica, Nicodemus, and Joseph of Arimathea, all in various attitudes of devotion, surprise, and glorification. Whilst they thus watch the Saviour, as He slowly ascends to heaven, the Chorus still sing the beautiful, heart-stirring strains of the hymn of victory, with its constant refrain of Hallelujahs:—

Preis Ihm, dem Todesüberwinder	Praise Him! the Conqueror of death,
Der einst verdammt auf Gabbatha!	Who once was doom'd on Gabbatha;
Preis Ihm dem Heiliger der Sünder,	Praise Him Who for all sinners hath
Der für uns starb auf Golgatha!	Bought life eterne on Golgotha!
Bringt Lob und Preis dem Höchsten dar,	Bring praise unto the One most high;
Dem Lamme, das getödtet war!	The Lamb Who for our sins did die!
Halleluja:	Hallelujah!
Das siegreich aus dem Grab hervor	Who, conquering, from the grave did rise,
Sich hebet im Triumph empor	Triumphant, mounting to the skies!
Halleluja! Halleluja!.	Hallelujah! He is risen!
Ja lasst des Bundes Harfe klingen,	Yea, let the harps of praise resound,
Dass Freude durch die Seele bebt!	Let joy through every spirit thrill!
Lasst uns dem Sieger Kronen bringen,	Let now the Victor's brow be crown'd,
Der auferstand und ewig lebt.	He's risen, and He liveth still!
Lobsinget alle Himmelsheere!	Hallelujah! He is risen!
Dem Herrn sei Ruhm und Herrlichkeit;	Ye heavenly hosts, your praises bring,
Anbetung, Macht und Kraft und Ehre	To Him all power and glory be;
Von Ewigkeit zu Ewigkeit!	His fame and adoration sing,
	From now unto eternity.
Bringt Lob und Preis dem Höchsten dar,	Bring praise unto the Lord most high,
Dem Lamme, das getödtet war!	The Lamb who for our sins did die!
Halleluja! Halleluja!	Hallelujah! He is risen!

Before the last refrain the falling curtain conceals the beautiful tableau, and the Schutzgeister, closing up on the proscenium, sing in exalted strains the final Hallelujah chorus. They then gather up their flowing robes, and,

ACT XVIII.—THE ASCENSION.

separating, slowly and gracefully leave the scene of their long and lofty task, whilst the audience, for the first time, are left alone to reflect on the marvellous things which they have witnessed during the long performance. Do the thousands of spectators return to their homes with spirits bowed down in sorrow at the thought of Christ's agony and death, or with joy in the strengthened assurance that in His glorious resurrection every believer has a sure pledge of his own future resurrection, and the earnest of eternal life, as promised by the Lord Himself at the institution of the Last Supper :—

Why are ye all so mournful, dearest children?
Why gaze so sadly on your Lord? Let not your hearts be troubled: ye believe in God,

Believe also in me.—My Father's house Hath many mansions, and I go before, There to prepare a dwelling unto you. And I will come again, and you will take Unto myself, that where I am ye be.

Many and beautiful lines have been written by visitors concerning the impressions which the play left upon them. We here reproduce a few: "Powerfully affected," says Knorr, "moved to the inmost depths of the soul, and yet wondrously elevated in feeling, does the spectator leave the theatre. What thoughts, what sentiments fill the breast of the returning visitor! How different from anything else that we have experienced are the impressions left by this play, so simple yet so powerful and grand!" Hermine von Patruban's beautiful words assuredly express the feelings of the majority of visitors, when she says : "We leave the theatre as we would a church after hearing a heart-stirring sermon or the liturgy during Passion Week."—"In deep silence," says Lady Herbert, "we left the solemn representation, and wended our way to the church, where we could best reflect on what we had seen, and pray that these impressions might never disappear from our mind and heart." "Yes, it was divine service," exclaims Dubbers, "and how wondrous a divine service it was! Filled with contentment to the inmost depth of the soul, the noblest yearnings stilled, and with calmed feelings, the spectator departs, having found everything which he had longed and sought for." With earnest mien, pondering on the scenes that have been witnessed, prince and peasant alike leave the theatre visibly affected by the events of that Divine Life which was sacrificed for the sake of all.

"Who has taught these simple minds this correct comprehension, this tenderness of feeling, which is so evident in all their *rôles* ?—this harmony, which does not detract from the glorious picture of the Redeemer as we believe on Him, but enables us to find in that maltreated innocence, in that reviled holiness, the Ideal so deeply impressed in our hearts?" asks Miss Patruban, and this writer answers : "It is the pure enthusiasm of believing minds, love of God, and of eternal truth," that has inspired the villagers in their labours. Having once witnessed the Passion Play, we no longer look upon it as an interesting relic of the distant past, out of keeping with the times, lingering on a threatened existence; but as upon the most marvellous and elevated dramatic exhibition of our epoch, and the perfection of the religious drama. Indeed, one can almost believe in witnessing the Play that he sees Christ descended to earth once more, preaching amid the sunny hills and valleys of Judea, living over the sad yet glorious events of His life among the men who misunderstood, persecuted and brutally pushed out of existence,—that life in whose sacrifice is hid the mystery of redemption and reconciliation. May God preserve and prosper this wondrous drama and the devoted village players, so that the Passion pilgrims of future centuries, like those of the present, may, on leaving the valley of the Ammer, repeat with the venerable Daisenberger:

> "Praise be to God! He hath this vale created
> To show to man the glory of His name;
> And these wide hills the Lord hath consecrated,
> Where He His love eternal may proclaim."

OBER-AMMERGAU BOOKS.
MUNICH (In Commission) WILLIAM HUMMEL.
TÜRKENSTRASSE NR. 20.

ALBUM
OF THE PASSION PLAY AT OBER-AMMERGAU (1871).

BEING sixty Photographs of the Scenes and Tableaux of the Passion Play, taken by command of His Majesty King Ludwig II. of Bavaria, by the Court Photographer, Albert, of Munich; and engravings on wood.

Introductory Chapters on the Rise, Development, and Decline of the Religious Drama, the Journey to the Passion-Play, the Village and People of Ober-Ammergau, the Story of the Play, a Description of the Ammergau Theatre, and a Full Account of the Passion-Play, with the Text and Songs of the Chorus,

By JOHN P. JACKSON,
MUNICH AND LONDON, 1874.

Dedicated by permission to His Majesty King Ludwig II. of Bavaria.

" Your request for permission to dedicate the 'Album of the Passion Play at Ober-Ammergau' to His Majesty the King has been most graciously received. His Majesty expressed repeatedly his especial pleasure in the work, which through a happy combination of word and illustration, gives a vivid representation of the Ammergau Passion Play; and he has authorized me to inform you that His Majesty accepts with pleasure the dedication of the work. "✱ ✱ ✱ EISENHART."

A few copies of this splendid work, which is entirely out of print, the royal permission having been granted only for two hundred sets of Photographs, may be had at the principal Book and Printsellers at Munich. Price M. 225.—£11 5s.

A limited number of this work, without the Photographs and Etchings, containing only the Text and the Engravings on Wood is for sale at the above Stores. Price M. 30.—£1 10s.

THE HOMES OF OBER-AMMERGAU.

A SERIES of twenty Etchings in Phototypes from the Original Pen and Ink Drawings, with Notes of a Diary kept during a three months' residence in Ober-Ammergau,
By ELIZA GREATOREX,
MUNICH AND NEW YORK, 1871.

On Sale in Munich and at Ober-Ammergau. Price M. 30.
Some of the Phototypes are to be had separately. Price M. 1.

A LIST OF WORKS ON THE PASSION PLAY.

Blackburn, Henry. Art in the Mountains. London, 1871, 1880.
Brunner, S. Das Passionsspiel zu O. A. 1860, 1870. Vienna, 1870.
Clarus, L. Das Passionsspiel zu Ober-Ammergau. Munich, 1860.
Daisenberger, Pastor. Geschichte des Dorfes Ober-A. Munich, 1858.
Daisenberger, Pastor, Jos. Alois. Bericht über das Passionsspiel zu Ober-Ammergau im Jahre 1850. (Deutinger's Collection of Reports.)
Daisenberger. Mahnungsworte des hochwürdigen Herrn Pfarrers J. A. Daisenberger am Tage vor der ersten Aufführung der Passions Vorstellungen gerichtet an die Gemeinde von Ober-A. (Sermon.) Munich, 1850.
Daisenberger, Pastor J. A. Die Früchte der Passionsbetrachtung, vorgestellt in fünf Predigten, welche zu Oberammergau in der heiligen Fastenzeit des Passionsjahres gehalten wurden. Regensburg, 1872.
Deutinger, Dr. Martin von. Das Passionsspiel in Oberammergau. (A collection of Reports on the Passion-Play.) Munich, 1851.
Devrient, Eduard. Geschichte der deutschen Schauspielkunst. Vol. I; Geschichte der Mittelalterlichen Schauspielkunst. Leipsic, 1848.
Devrient, Edward. Ueber das Passionsspiel im Dorfe O.-A. Leipsic, 1880. Second edition.
Dubbers, W. Das Oberammergauer Passionsspiel nach seiner geschichtlichen, künstlerischen und culturhistorischen Bedeutung. Frankf., 1872.
Görres, Guido. Das Theater im Mittelalter und das Passionsspiel in Oberammergau. Deutinger's Collection, 1840.
Hase, Dr. Karl. Miracle Plays and Sacred Dramas : an Historical Survey. Translated from the German by A. W. Jackson, and Edited by the Rev. W. W. Jackson, Fellow of Exeter College, Oxford, 1880.
Holland, Dr. Hyacinth. Das Ammergauer Passionsspiel im Jahre 1870. Munich, 1871. Die Entwickelung des deutschen Theaters im Mittelalter und das Ammergauer Passionsspiel. Munich, 1871.
Howitt-Watts, Mrs. An Art Student in Munich. London.
Knorr, Emil. Entstehung und Entwickelung der geistlichen Schauspiele in Deutschland und das Passionsspiel in Oberammergau. Leipsic, 1872.
Mac Coll, Rev. M. The Ober-Ammergau Passion-Play, with Introduction on Origin and Development of Miracle Plays. London, 1871, 1880.
Oxenham, H. N. Recollections of Ober-Ammergau in 1871. Lond., 1871, 1880.
Patruban, Hermine von. Erinnerung an O.-A., 1870. Vienna, 1871.
Pichler, Adolf. Ueber das Drama des Mittelalters in Tyrol. Innsb., 1850.
Seguin, G. G. The Country of the Passion Play. London, 1880.]

The Co-operative Metropolitan Laundries,
LIMITED.

Incorporated under the Companies' Acts, 1862 and 1867, whereby the liability of each Shareholder is limited to amount subscribed.

Capital, £15,000, in 15,000 Shares of £1 each.

Payable, 10s. on Application, and 10s. on Allotment, all further liability ceasing. With power to increase.

FIRST ISSUE, 5,000 SHARES AT PAR.

Directors.
AUGUSTO SOARES, Esq., *Chairman*, 54½, Bishopsgate Street, E.C.
LIEUTENANT-COLONEL HOBSON, Thistle Grove, S.W.
BARON DE-WOLFFERS, 63, Fleet Street, E.C.
EDWARD POWELL, Esq., 18, Queen Victoria Street, E.C.

Bankers.
THE UNION BANK OF LONDON, 2, Princes Street, E.C.

Solicitor.
JOHN ANDREWS, Esq., 45, Fenchurch Street, E.C.

Auditors.
MESSRS. FOSTER HIGHT & CO., 3, Copthall Buildings, E.C.

Secretary.
STUART BARNES, Esq.

Offices.
3, MILDMAY CHAMBERS, OLD BROAD STREET, E.C.

Works.
No. 1 LAUNDRY: No. 205, RICHMOND ROAD, HACKNEY.

PROSPECTUS.

This Company has been formed to supply a want long felt, and frequently expressed, by the public, viz.: the establishment of Laundries on the Co-operative principle.

The unparalleled success which has attended all well-managed Co-operative Societies, and the benefits which have accrued to the Members, lead to the just inference that the present movement, which presents unusual facilities for Co-operation, will be attended with similar results.

Although a Laundry is an industry connected with a branch of domestic economy of almost universal necessity, up to the present time it has scarcely been touched on a large scale, the cleansing of linen being for the most part entrusted to persons with limited accommodation, living and working in houses neither healthy nor clean.

London is far behind Continental and American Cities as regards Laundry work; in the latter especially there are large establishments, conducted upon the best principles, under proper sanitary arrangements and practical supervision, which insure immunity from the spread of infection, prevent irregularities, and save annoyance and trouble to Customers.

Dr. Richardson, the well-known authority on matters relating to health and Sanitary Science, writing in the "Gentleman's Magazine" for April last, makes the following statement on this point :—

"The want now most felt amongst the educated, in our large centres, is the means for getting a due supply of well-washed clean clothes. In London, at this moment, a thousand public laundries are wanted, before that cleanliness which is next to godliness can ever be recognized by the apostles of health who feel that their mission in the world stands second only on the list of goodly and godly labours for mankind."

To supply this want, the Directors propose to open Laundries in every District of London upon the basis above named, availing themselves of all means for the saving of time and labour in carrying out their work. They propose adopting a new and most efficient method for thoroughly cleansing the material, without the use of injurious chemicals, and unnecessary wear and tear of rubbing.

The mode adopted will be thoroughly disinfecting.

The profits arising from the Laundry as worked in the ordinary way are known to be considerable. The outlay required, compared with the return, is small, and when work is conducted upon a large scale, with well-arranged machinery, efficient management, and proper supervision, the profits will greatly increase with but a small addition to the expenditure.

The first Laundry, situate near the London Fields, Hackney, has been obtained upon very advantageous terms, and is now in full operation, with a daily increasing business. All the advantages of co-operation will be secured to shareholders, who will in addition to the benefit of the low charges (as per tariff enclosed) *secure first a dividend of* 10 *per cent.* on capital subscribed, and also a return from surplus profits *pro râta* according to amount of expenditure.

Practical and experienced managers will be in charge of every department, and the works under careful supervision, thus securing to patrons full satisfaction by prompt execution of orders.

The Directors call special attention to the fact that the Capital of the Company has been divided into £1 Shares, to place the investment within the reach of all classes, and thus secure certain success and large profits. Shares must be applied for on the supplied form, and left at the Bankers, with deposit, or forwarded to the Secretary.

Full particulars may be obtained from the Solicitor, Secretary, or the Managers at the Works.

www.ingramcontent.com/pod-product-compliance
Lightning Source LLC
Chambersburg PA
CBHW031354160426
43196CB00007B/808